MOIN SIDDIQUI

Deliverance

This edition first published in paperback by
Michael Terence Publishing in 2024
www.mtp.agency

ISBN 9781800947948

Cover design
Michael Terence Publishing

Michael Terence
Publishing

1

Ever since the creation of man – there has been a prophet sent down to teach them the way of the living. The last prophet who graced the Earth was Prophet Muhammad (P.B.U.H), who spread Islam throughout the Earth.

Prophet Muhammad spread the word of God through Islam, and his own words were known as the Hadeeth.

It was the truth in the Hadeeth in which Austin found comfort. Austin had converted to Islam free of choice and the most comfort he found in was the truth of the Hadeeth which told the mirage journey of the prophet to heaven and hell.

In this journey, angel Gabriel had accompanied the prophet through the skies. When they had reached hell, the prophet saw that it was occupied by more women than men. He asked Angel Gabriel the reason behind this and the angel replied, "The women were ungrateful to their husbands."

It struck true for Austin because he was already divorced once. He had married young but his wife had left him when he was broke and couldn't make ends meet even though he did everything in his power to provide for her.

Austin used to work at a textile factory but he didn't earn much. To make ends meet, he found work as navy in Liverpool docks. There was shortage of labour so he was asked to supply men to help the progress. In over six months, he was supplying around fifty men. At that point, having divorced his wife, he wasn't overly concerned about the revenue. He only wanted to ensure that the work was carried out successfully to the right specifications.

Austin studied through Abrahamic religions before reaching for Islam. During this time period, he found out about the Ten Commandments and Prophet Musa, who was traditionally considered the intermediary through whom these commandments were delivered to the Israelites. According to the biblical accounts in the Book of Exodus and the Book of Deuteronomy, Musa received the Ten Commandments directly from God on Mount Sinai.

He read that it was during the 1500 year BCE when a bush was burned on a mountain to attract an old man's attention at the bottom of the hill. His intention was to find grass for his sheep to graze as he slowly climbed the hill, but his age had let him down.

He sat down and looked around, hoping he could see grass as going down hill would be far easier.

The old man was startled when he realised that the bush which was on fire wasn't just another bush burning due to dry and hot weather experienced in the desert, rather there was an angel standing next to the now burnt out bush.

"Musa!" an equally old man called out from the bottom of the hill.

"I can't hear you," Musa replied pointing to his ears. The man at the bottom of the hill was Haroon. He knew that Moses stuttered and it may take him time to reply.

At the foot of the hill an old lady joined Haroon. She was crying but managed to say, "Come Haroon, the people are worshiping a gold cow."

Haroon looked at her in confusion. He asked, "How did they make a gold cow?"

"From the gold you gave them for safe keeping," she replied as she sniffled.

Haroon looked on at Musa and said to the old lady, "Zipporah, please tell Musa not to climb any further."

Zipporah shook her head, "He's a stubborn old man and hard of hearing. It's best to leave him alone. He goes up there for days at a time and says he's looking for grass for the sheep to graze. I think he goes up there to escape people who make fun of his stuttering and deafness." She was quiet for a moment, then said, "What do I tell the people who are dancing around the calf?"

Haroon sighed, "Tell them to offer food and drink. I am sure my brother goes up there for a reason."

"What's the reason?" Zipporah asked, not understanding Musa's doings at all.

"I don't know, but recently he has been talking about one God and asking why the tribe is dancing around fires," Haroon replied as Musa continued walking up the mountains.

When Musa felt tired he sat down and looked up into the sky. Haroon and Zipporah looked on with different levels of care and confusion.

"See, look at him. It looks like he is searching for something or someone," Zipporah commented.

"Can't believe Musa was once a prince of Egypt," Haroon replied.

"The life we could've had, would've been a life of luxury. Now we're stuck here in the middle of nowhere and watching people dance around a cow. Wasting food and water which we don't have much of."

"Patience, I know my brother and he has a reason to be up there."

"He is nearly eighty years old and for the last forty years he has been in the wilderness. He needs to calm down before he loses his mind," Zipporah spoke her mind.

But Haroon defended his brother, "No, his mind is still sharp, he stutters a bit and a bit deaf."

Zipporah sighed, "I just hope he calms down and stops wandering off to the hills."

"Before he went off he was saying something about that first universe was created and it made God very angry," Haroon looked up again.

Musa had now become a speckle in the distance and Haroon had to squint his eyes to see his figure. Yesterday, two people had died near the edge of the hill and although Musa saw the decomposed bodies, he didn't agree to the reason of their demise. He pulled his attention to his brother who was a distant figure. From the corner of his eye, he saw a plume of smoke. Still, a quick glance still didn't confirm where it was originating from.

"I wonder what the tribe is doing?" Zipporah questioned.

"It keeps them busy making statues to remind them of God."

"And the dancing?"

"It's the devil in them against God."

"But I love dancing."

"Has it got something to do with putting the devil in front of God?"

"Maybe you're overthinking the issue. It is possible to just dance for fun."

"Maybe you're right, but probably wrong."

As the morning entered the afternoon, Musa had looked tired as the sun started to cast a shadow. A crow flew by and Musa looked up startled. Within seconds the crow had disappeared, taking its shadow with speed.

"I wonder what my husband is doing up there?" Zipporah asked again.

"Probably looking for answers."

"Answers to what exactly?"

"Power of God I presume."

"Hasn't this been going on for a few years now?"

"Try a few decades."

"What about his forefathers?"

"What about them?"

"Well, he keeps going about Adam."

"Oh him, that's how it all started."

"Everyone keeps calling him Moses Loses," Zipporah said, feeling disgruntled for the sake of her husband.

Meanwhile Moses was still on the mountain, considering sitting down and thinking about his marriage.

This part of the event was very interesting for Austin because while Zipporah was worried about what her husband was doing, Moses' first thought was to think about whether they had a bad marriage. He thought of how their family never ate together. Then he thought that the children were undesirable and undisciplined. His third thought was that the family never went anywhere anymore. Musa wandered for forty years in the wilderness and his final thought was that they always argued.

The relentless heat was similar to a bad marriage, that to avoid getting sunburnt was to get out of the bad marriage. Austin knew that to be true, hence he had left his first wife.

"Is that what God bought him to talk about?" Musa thought.

"God isn't a marriage counsellor," he thought again.

Haroon watched the tribe from a distance and he could just hear the sound of the drums.

As Moses climbed further, he knew that his eyes had spots like floating crystals. His sole focus was on God and nothing else. Austin was moved deeply by his devotion to God. While the Israelites continued to whirl in the wilderness, Moses kept his eyes fixed on one thing – God. Even with each unsettling circumstances, his knees never buckled. And he found God in the end, at Mount Sinai as God covered it in clouds for six says straight and on the seventh day, the Lord called to Musa from inside the cloud. The Israelites saw the glory of the Lord resembling that of a blazing fire at the mountain's summit.

Prophet Musa's love for God and his unrelenting effort to find God was what motivated Austin to do the same.

After this, he studied Islam before converting. In his studies, he came across the meaning of "lut" which was during the time of Sodom. During Ibrahim and Lut's migration to Palestine, they received the divine decree of Allah that Lut had been chosen as a Prophet and Messenger for the people of Sodom. Allah instructed the new Prophet to travel to the city of Sodom, located on the border of Jordan and Palestine, and summon the transgressors back to the worship of Allah.

Sodom was a thriving city that was visited by many travellers, merchants and businessmen for trade. However, Sodom was also the most corrupt city with the highest criminal activity during that time. Travellers passing Sodom were often waylaid and robbed of their belongings, and sometimes were mercilessly murdered. But, the most notorious act of evil that was committed by this corrupt nation was homosexuality.

Homosexuality was introduced into the world by the people of Lut—none in the history of mankind had ever experienced or practiced homosexuality before Sodom. This shameful practice was the norm amongst this nation, and the entire population engaged in it. They were immensely proud of their conduct, spoke openly about it, and engaged in these immoral behaviors out in the open.

Prophet Lut soon settled in Sodom and began to devise ways to bring his people into the fold of Islam. He was well-aware that his nation was the most corrupt nation of that time; but he held firm faith and hoped and prayed that they would soon see the error of their ways and enter into the path of Allah.

They were immensely proud of their conduct, spoke openly about it, and engaged in these immoral behaviors out in the open.

One day, three handsome men walked into Sodom disguised as angels to help Lut fight homosexuality. The angel's first magically blinded the men as they pounded the door to find the handsome and beautiful looking men. Then once blinded, the Lord showered hot clay boulders from the sky.

The Dead Sea lay at the site of the corrupt city of Sodom, and remains as a powerful reminder of Allah's wrath against the people of Prophet Lut.

Austin learned a lot from the story of Prophet Lut as it underscored the responsibility of prophets to guide their communities toward righteousness.

Austin asked an engineer he worked with who looked smart and beautiful, "Do you know the Prophet Lut?"

"No, should I?" the engineer asked rhetorically.

"You remind me of the era of Sodom where men were all homosexuals," Austin commented.

"Hang on a minute Austin, I know Liverpool is bad, but not that bad," the engineer joked.

As the two men walked together towards the excavation zone, marked with plastic water-filled barriers, rain started to fall in a drizzle.

On reflection, Austin was a quiet man at home in Chapel-Le-Firth and was married to a brunette who was twenty-three years younger than him. To outsiders, he was the luckiest man in Derbyshire. However, in reality he was embroiled in difficulties that normally came with a trophy wife. Rihanna was a half-caste. She was a mixture of German father and Syrian mother. A mixture of atheist father and a Muslim mother created a cocktail of explosive arguments at the slightest issue of religion. With such a mixture of differences in cultures, religions, and beliefs, Rihanna was not only a trophy wife, but a wife bordering on the Champions League and European Cup. It could easily be said that with her measurements of 38-26-36 many men would have put her as a World Cup trophy.

However, Rihanna's parents found it difficult to arrange a marriage for her as that was what her mother wanted. Her father wanted her to play the field and find a husband for herself. Her physique of 152 centimetre height created a gravity issue as she would fall over quite easily and with a shoe size of three, her centre of gravity was frequently positioned outside the stomach line of balance. Her facial features reflected her physique with a long nose, thin lips, and a thin face.

Truth be told, it was difficult for Austin to visit shops, supermarkets or restaurants. Anywhere where there were men. The problem was that Austin was addicted to nicotine and on many occasions he would go out of a restaurant to have a cigarette, only to find a man trying to talk to Rihanna. Visiting pubs and clubs wasn't ever an option.

Rihanna's skin colour was like a seasoned olive bordering on gold. And when she got ready for Austin, he would ask her to tone down the colours. Her choice of lip colour was changed to light pink and her eye-shadow to slightly pink. He would ask her not to wear eyelashes. Depending on the time of the day, men would be equally attracted at night time after nine. Austin would schedule the outing so by nine they would be safely back in their mansion of eight bedrooms.

In their mansion, the two bedrooms were occupied by their two sons, aged twenty-one and eleven, leaving six bedrooms for the parents to choose from. Austin chose the one overlooking the field and Rihanna chose the closest one to her sons.

The choice of different sleeping arrangements was by mutual consent, but not understood by their eleven-year-old son. However, the elder son somewhat accepted the change for the last three years. Both sons supported Liverpool whilst Austin supported Chelsea. Rihanna had no preference of who won between the two teams. She was more interested in trying to keep peace for the ninety minutes between father and sons.

It wasn't always easy, especially when the two boys turned a discussion of tactics into arguments and then a brawl in the middle of the TV lounge. Most of the time it was the younger son who would come out with Austin, waging a twenty-pound bet with Rihanna.

Austin's life was a journey of many ups and downs, but the most important part of his journey was his path to finding God after researching and reading on his own. He had found the one God – Allah – as there are no other Gods before or after him.

2

In Islam, the idea of the Hereafter is one that is often used to promise Muslims things they will be rewarded for if they follow their religion as is told by Allah and spread by the Messenger, the Prophet Muhammad (P.B.U.H). It is to encourage Muslims to remain on the right path and follow the Quran and Hadeeth.

Immersing oneself in the worship of Allah is the sign of a great Muslim, however, there is also the concept of balancing worldly life and spiritual life in Islam. The religions also provides guidance on how Muslims should navigate their lives to achieve a harmonious balance between their worldly responsibilities and spiritual obligations.

This was a concept that Austin was wholly impressed by in his studies of Islam. Because apart from being a Muslim, he and his family were essentially also just human beings living along with the current world affairs.

If Austin were to see his own family dynamics, he and Rihanna had a regular family. The two boys fought at least twice a year when Liverpool played Chelsea and, occasionally, three when the two teams played in the FA Cup.

Austin remembered during this one FA Cup game, he had wagered a ten-pound bet with the boys and the usual twenty-pound bet with Rihanna. A fight broke out amongst them as the game went on and Rihanna prayed that Liverpool would win the FA Cup. The boys won that

Saturday afternoon of course, but the fights were just short of Cain and Able outcome. It was a miracle that the eldest son's dream was to save the planet by developing a microchip that controlled the disposal of vapes correctly to avoid disposable vapes ending up in a landfill.

Single-handed, Harry Brady ended up developing a microchip that would eventually save the planet and re-cycle the lithium batteries to power the cars. Austin had placed a bet with Rihanna, which was a one hundred pound wager whether a US-based investment bank would agree with Harry on an investment of one million dollars. When it actually ended up happening, their younger son, Alan, stopped the fights with his elder brother.

Allan's chubby face took more of a serious tone and suddenly the arguments turned to serious discussions. Austin won the bet once again by hedging against his firstborn.

Due to this, Austin and Rihanna moved together in the third master bedroom of their house as Austin was right about his son against Rihanna's prediction that Harry wouldn't amount to much. That was five years ago and he promised Rihanna that he wouldn't touch her beautiful body until Harry proved Rihanna wrong.

However, light pecks on the cheeks were allowed, to keep the two boys from asking questions. Rihanna referred the boys to the song "Endless Love" to describe her marriage to Austin. The father referred to the song "Winner Takes It All." When he won the bet, Austin ran around the room with his win as if it was the World Cup.

Austin loved these moments with his family the most. It gave him an out from the world out there. He had his religion and his family, and having them both made all the difference in the world. Before he was a family man and devoted servant of Allah, he had felt life to be very lacking. There had been an overwhelming sense if isolation that he felt wherever he went, like the souls residing in him was searching for something more.

He was surrounded by a sea of faces, each engrossed in their own worlds. This feeling of not having done enough left him yearning for a deeper connection that eluded him.

Even though life had been tough at times, Austin had never given up hope. He didn't have a great job, his first wife left him, and even then he kept going on. Once he was successful as a contractor and he had everything he essentially needed, what was left for him to do? He had no wife and no kids to take care of. He felt like he was adrift, just doing what was asked of him and nothing more.

Austin had achieved everything with pure will, but after that, life had turned monotonous. Now, he looked around at his life after finding Allah and Islam, it felt like this was what was missing in his life. After he accepted the word of Allah, life started to make sense on its own. He met Rihanna, got married and had two kids. Life felt like it finally had some colours to it. Like it was finally moving forward instead of being stuck in one place.

But it wouldn't have happened if he didn't take the time to understand what was missing from his life. It was the guidance of a spiritual kind. A connection deeper than he had ever experienced before.

Austin felt that everywhere he went now. And he felt it in the moment, walking with another colleague of his who was also a contractor. The silence between them had made

Austin think back on his journey and how grateful he was to be there at that moment in time. He loved doing the job he had and he always made sure that the guys around him knew that he was someone they could talk to, any time they needed. He loved talking to people who shared his passion for engineering.

He turned to Ubaid, his new co-worker, and realised he did not know much about the guy.

Hence, Austin decided to take matters into his own hands.

"So who do you support Ubaid?" he asked the young bearded engineer.

"Kabul Bank AFC," Ubaid replied proudly.

Austin raised a brow, "Which league are they in?"

"Afghanistan Premier League," Ubaid replied with a shrug.

"I didn't realise Afghanistan had a premier league."

Ubaid's smile was grim when he replied, "No one really knows Afghanistan as a free country."

Austin nodded slowly, then added, "I know they beat Russia."

"They also beat the United States and Britain."

"I presume they did," Austin commented.

"Not presume-they did."

As they approached the vast excavation, Ubaid phone started ringing and he stopped to answer a phone call. Austin couldn't hear the conversation and even if he did it was in a different language. Ubaid then switched the phone off and told Austin he had a headache and was going home.

Austin asked if everything was all right and he informed Austin that his son had just farted and his wife was worried. Austin raised both of his brows until they touched his hairline. Austin realised straight away that the young engineer wasn't interested in the work or remotely concerned about the project. Ubaid did not say anything further and Austin did not dare ask. He swiftly returned to his car and drive away.

Experience of life had taught him that people worked for success of the project or their personal bank balance, and they wanted to have all that without having to do any work. Being at work was a great measure of a person, especially a great measure of an engineer was to stay on site and look down a hole and resolve problems there and then.

Austin soon realised that Ubaid was that kind of a person, which was completely opposite of who Austin was as a person. Ubaid never returned to work that day and Austin made his own decisions about the rising water level and sandy clay eroding by the hour. That decision was to install due watering system five metres from the edge of the excavation and continually pumping water into a culvert some fifty meters away.

Instead of the project being design and build it became a build and design. Austin had taken a risk of not getting paid, but it was choice of losing one of his workers or the bank giving way or stopping work and there was a chance of having a flood like in times of Noah, which were the floods that killed all the sinners and saved the believers.

Like Austin, Noah was a tiller of the soil and a drinker of wine. Austin loved working the ground and a few drinks after work. The flood in the excavation was reversal of God's creation to show how powerful water is in its elementary state of two hydrogen and one oxygen atoms. Austin questioned how these two elements came together in the creation of the seas. The promise of God that he will never send another flood. With his belief in mind, Austin knew that the ground water was controllable.

He reminisced about his ex-wife and how she was uncontrollable, unlike the ground water. He supposed people were like that when they remained unchecked – at least in their eyes.

His former wide was forever trying to manipulate people through her evil eyes. She had a lazy eye, and rest of her wasn't much better either.

When he had met Rihanna, his first impression had not been all that, but the fact that she had made an impression was a big deal because Austin was used to the kind of women that his previous wife was and he was not going to be getting fooled another time.

Austin had met Rihanna in a nightclub in Buxton, Derbyshire. Rihanna had been ditched by her husband because she claimed that her father-in-law attempted to rape her. Austin was already shocked by her beauty, but he was also shocked by the event as Rihanna unfolded the story and told him about how it all went down.

"My husband was a drug addict," she had started, pausing for a second to look around to see if anyone was listening.

"A Liverpool supporter?" Austin asked, leaning toward her. He was not going to lie, he was already taken with her on that first meeting.

"One of them," she replied as Austin pretended to spit. Then continued, "It was an arranged marriage."

Austin nodded before asking, "Do you mean a forced marriage?"

Rihanna shook her head, "No, a forced marriage is different. An arranged marriage is when the bride finds the groom attractive."

Austin did not know much about these principles because he had not grown up in a society that was brimming with arranged marriages. The Western culture was vastly different than what Rihanna had possibly grown up in.

Still, Austin was curious to know, hence he responded, "And did you?"

Rihanna nodded sagely, "Oh yeah, he was perfect. We were a very attractive couple."

Austin hummed, thoughtful, "So? What happened?" Austin leaned forward to listen as he was slightly deaf in both ears.

"On the wedding night, he had been snorting cocaine and couldn't consummate the marriage. So he used marital aid," Rihanna confided.

Austin arched a brow, "What he couldn't do the honour?"

"Honour?" asked a confused Rihanna.

"You're not from around here, are you?"

Rihanna shook her head, "Pakistan."

"Oh, a terrorist," Austin remarked carelessly.

Rihanna narrowed her eyes at him, "No, I'm not a tourist."

Austin replied calmly, "Terrorist love, not tourist. You know with AK47 and bombs."

Rihanna looked at him like he was an imbecile. She went on to explain that Muslim men who didn't honour their wives didn't actually honour Allah. Islam – contrary to popular belief – had actually given women a lot of power and safety, especially when the Prophet was born into a society where women were treated horribly.

Austin contemplated Rihanna's words a lot and questioned to himself whether her husband was actually straight, or whether he was a homosexual, because who could look at the angelic face of Rihanna and reject her?

He offered to hug Rihanna after hearing her story and whilst she agreed, Austin wanted to ask her if they could spend the night together. He whispered his question delicately in her left ear.

"That's not possible," Rihanna replied.

So Austin started to kiss her ear, licking the top of the ear and biting it.

Rihanna moaned and suddenly shrugged away. She ran into the other room and firmly shut the door.

Austin moved closer to the door, ensuring he stood at least a metre away from the door.

"I just wanted to say I'm sorry," shouted Austin.

There was no reply. Austin tried very hard to listen to any response but was let down as he was deaf in his right ear.

He realised there were only two possibilities for the outcome.

The first favourable outcome would be that she would invite him into her room.

The second unfavourable outcome would be that she would report him for attempted rape.

Attempted rape occurred when an individual attempts to commit the act of rape but failed to carry out the full offence. In other words, an individual can be said to have committed attempted rape if they have made an attempt to intentionally provoke a sexual response without the person's consent, without success.

This could be for several reasons, for example, the victim fighting the individual off, the prevention of the individual from doing so by a third party, or the perpetrator withdrawing from the attempt after changing their mind. Despite the failure to commit the full offence, attempted rape is treated the same as the full offence of rape and the sentencing guidelines are subsequently similar.

Austin was aware of the punishment for the offence. If the prosecution can prove that an individual had the intent and has committed an act that can be considered as more than merely preparatory, then the defendant will be found guilty of attempted rape and sentenced accordingly. As is common for most offences under the Criminal Attempts Act 1981, sentencing guidelines for attempted rape are similar to that for the commission of the full offence.

Austin stood there, waiting patiently and after a while, the door opened. Rihanna peeked about from the opening and asked for Austin to enter the small room which contained a Queen-sized bed.

Austin still had no clue regarding what was going on or what Rihanna was actually thinking. He was fearful, but he was also hopeful as she entered the room behind her and shut the door quietly.

He stood, facing her as she stood facing away from him. Austin felt like Rihanna was also doing a lot of thinking, it was obvious by the wringing of her hands and the chewing of her cuticles.

She finally turned around and Austin's hope blossomed. Rihanna asked him to sit down on the bed. He followed obligingly and comfortably settled on the bed. He was patient and waited for Rihanna to come to terms with her decision, whatever it may be.

He wasn't there to pressurize her and he was going to leave as soon as she asked him to leave, but Rihanna wasn't asking him to leave.

She came closer and took a seat beside him on the bed and he could smell her more properly now.

As they turned to one another, both of them had not realised that it was the start of something neither of them expected that night.

3

Islam places significant importance on the holistic well-being of individuals, including their mental and emotional states. Islam considers human beings as holistic entities, encompassing physical, spiritual, and mental dimensions. The well-being of an individual is interconnected, and attention to mental health is seen as integral to achieving overall balance and wholeness.

When Austin found out about this, he realized that the mental health of the workers also played an important part in the efficiency of the output. He decided to take on a therapist whose name was Stephanie Bader. She was a short, slim, beautiful, professional, middle-aged brunette.

Stephanie started to send templates of the pre-assessment questionnaire asking the employees to complete it before their assessment. She told Austin, "I need to understand their requirements and prepare an action plan based on the pre-assessment, practical assessment, and if need be, a referral to a third GP."

Austin agreed in principle, but couldn't actually see it working in practice. He was aware of mental health as his ex-wife was diagnosed with bipolar disorder and had transgressing issues since the age of eighteen. Her general appearance was always clothes that she hadn't changed for weeks. Her nail colour was stained with tobacco because she smoked heavily and her hair was always a mess. Her posture was uncomfortable and she walked very slowly by dragging her feet. He hoped that she was being taken care of now and was happy somewhere far off because clearly he hadn't been doing her any favours.

Austin had realised that being closely associated with religion had turned him into a kinder person than he was. These days, he felt more deeply about the people he perhaps should not be caring about at all.

The world is crumbling as the days pass by because the humans living in it are not as kind to each other as they should be. We hate each other and wage wars against the weak all because of what? There is always a reason that makes people lose all of their will and it has to do with money almost always.

A few days ago his eldest son phoned him to say that there was another episode related to the Gaza war and Austin started to look into the issue of what could possibly cause the relapse and found that the root cause of the war was ethnic cleansing based on gas reserves being found in Gaza Marine.

In the year 2000, natural gas reserves were discovered off the coast of the Gaza Strip as part of the licensing agreement granted by the Palestinian National Authority to British Gas. The identified gas field, named Gaza Marine, was of moderate size; however, during that period, it was viewed as a potential catalyst for enhancing the Palestinian economy and fostering regional cooperation.

Following the Hamas takeover of the Gaza Strip in 2007, the prospects for developing the gas field dwindled significantly. This was primarily due to the strained relationship with the Ramallah administration and Israel's refusal to engage with the Hamas group. The situation worsened with the discovery of substantial gas fields in

Israeli economic waters in 2009 and 2010, making Israel an improbable customer for Palestinian gas. As of early 2015, the development of Gaza's natural gas, as well as most of the Levantine gas, remained stalled.

On November 8, 1999, the Palestinians entered into a memorandum of intent with British Gas and a company associated with the Palestinian Authority, the Consolidated Contractors Company. This agreement granted them the right to explore the designated area. The identified natural gas reserve was estimated to be 35 BCM, surpassing the size of Israel's Yam Tethys maritime gas field. This discovery encompassed two smaller gas fields known as Gaza Marine 1 and Gaza Marine 2.

In 1999, Israeli Prime Minister Ehud Barak unilaterally set aside the exploration of Gaza's offshore resources for a potential future Palestinian state, without prior consultation stipulated with Israel. According to Michael Schwartz, Barak deployed the Israeli navy in Gaza's coastal waters to obstruct the implementation of the terms outlined in the modest contract between the Palestinian Authority and British Gas (BG) for the development of Gaza's Mediterranean gas resources. Israel insisted that the Gaza gas should be transported to facilities within its territory, at a price below the prevailing market rate, and that Israel should have control over all the (relatively modest) revenues allocated to the Palestinians to prevent the funds from being used to "fund terror."

According to Schwartz, this Israeli action marked the official demise of the Oslo Accords. By deeming Palestinian control over gas revenues unacceptable, the Israeli government committed itself to rejecting even the most limited form of Palestinian budgetary autonomy, let alone full sovereignty. Schwartz contends that, given this stance and the unlikelihood of any Palestinian entity agreeing to such terms, a future marred by armed conflict became inevitable.

The Israeli veto prompted British Prime Minister Tony Blair to intervene, attempting to broker an agreement that could appease both the Israeli government and the Palestinian Authority. The outcome was a 2007 proposal that aimed to deliver the gas to Israel rather than Egypt, at prices below the market rate. The agreement included a provision for the Palestinian Authority to eventually receive a 10% share of the revenues. However, these funds were initially directed to the Federal Reserve Bank in New York for future distribution, ensuring that they would not be utilized for attacks on Israel.

The Israelis cited the 2006 victory of the Islamist Hamas party in Palestinian elections as a deal-breaker. Despite Hamas agreeing to let the Federal Reserve supervise all spending, the Israeli government, under the leadership of Ehud Olmert at the time, insisted on not paying "royalties to the Palestinians." Instead, they proposed delivering the equivalent funds "in goods and services."

The offer was refused by the Hamas-led Palestinian unity government. Subsequently, Olmert imposed a blockade on Gaza, described by Israel's defense minister as a form of '"economic warfare"' intended to generate a political crisis, leading to a popular uprising against Hamas. With Egyptian cooperation, Israel took control of commerce in and out of Gaza, restricting even food imports and eliminating its fishing industry. Dov Weisglass, an advisor to Olmert, characterized this policy as putting the Palestinians "on a diet." According to the Red Cross, this blockade resulted in "chronic malnutrition," particularly among Gazan children.

As Moshe Ya'alon explained, "Hamas… has confirmed its capability to bomb Israel's strategic gas and electricity installations… It is clear that, without an overall military operation to uproot Hamas control of Gaza, no drilling work can take place without their consent."

In 2010-11, the Israeli government led by Prime Minister Netanyahu grappled with an energy crisis triggered by disruptions in 40% of Israel's gas supplies during the Arab Spring events in Egypt. The resulting surge in energy prices played a role in sparking some of the largest protests among Jewish Israelis in decades.

To safeguard Israel's northern gas fields from potential Hezbollah rocket attacks, the Iron Dome system was deployed near the Gaza border. This defensive system was tested during Operation Returning Echo, the fourth Israeli military effort aimed at weakening Hamas and eliminating any Palestinian "capability to bomb Israel's strategic gas and electricity installations."

Subsequent negotiations faced hurdles as Palestinians rejected Israel's demand for control over all fuel and revenues destined for Gaza and the West Bank. The newly formed Palestinian Unity government then took a cue from Lebanon, Syria, and Turkish Cypriots, signing an "exploration concession" with Gazprom, a major Russian natural gas company, in late 2013. Similar to Lebanon and Syria, the presence of the Russian Navy was seen as a potential deterrent to Israeli "interference."

In 2015, the Palestinian government reopened negotiations on the agreement with BG and revoked the exclusive rights granted to the company. Additionally, it increased the Palestinian Investment Fund (PIF) share from 10%, as stipulated in the previous agreement, to 17.5%. Following this, Shell acquired BG on April 8, 2016.

By 2017, the licenses for the Gaza Marine field were held by PIF with 17.5% of the development rights, Consolidated Contractors Company owning 27.5% of these rights, and Shell possessing 55%. The rights to develop and extract gas were solely under Palestinian ownership. In 2018, Shell, which had taken over British Gas, decided to relinquish its 60% stake in Gaza Marine, transferring it to Palestinian state-owned companies.

Often referred to simply as 'gas,' natural gas is a gaseous fossil fuel predominantly composed of methane. It is found in oil fields, natural gas fields, and coal beds (as coalbed methane). Before being used as a fuel, natural gas undergoes extensive processing to eliminate almost all materials other than methane.

Natural gas plays a significant role in electricity generation, especially when high efficiencies are achieved by combining gas turbines with a steam turbine in a combined cycle mode. In comparison to other fossil fuels, natural gas combustion is cleaner, emitting approximately 30% less carbon dioxide than oil and about 45% less than coal per unit of energy released. It is anticipated that natural gas reserves will reach their peak around 2030, roughly two decades after peak oil production. Compressed natural gas serves as a cleaner alternative to conventional automobile fuels like gasoline and diesel. Additionally, natural gas is commonly used for household cooking and central heating.

However, a primary challenge in the utilization of natural gas lies in its transportation and storage due to its low density. While pipeline transport is cost-effective, it becomes impractical for transoceanic transport. Liquefied natural gas can be transported in LNG carriers, but the necessary liquefaction facilities contribute to the overall cost. The practice of flaring gas during petroleum recovery, which adds to greenhouse gas emissions, is now prohibited in numerous countries.

This increase in the intensity of Israel's attack on Gaza can be connected back to them wanting control over assets that would make them more money in the future.

Money is something that some people can never have enough of. That was the thing with Austin's ex-wife. She wanted him to make more but did not stick around to see that happening as she was too impatient.

After Austin started talking with Stephanie, he couldn't help but think about his ex-wife and how she had struggled mentally. He asked Stephanie to make his ex-wife her first trial and see if she could help her for the sake of the children, who were now adults and in their thirties.

Stephanie asked his ex-wife if she was taking her prescribed medication and she replied, "I don't care anymore and want to join the thousands of Palestinians that are dying every day and going to heaven."

Stephanie stated to her that there are things individuals can control and the rest was controlled by political power.

"You may initially be diagnosed with clinical depression before you have a manic episode, after which you may be diagnosed with bipolar disorder," Stephanie said to Austin. Then Stephanie continued in earnest, "During an episode of depression, you may have overwhelming feelings of worthlessness, which can potentially lead to thoughts of suicide."

Austin replied, "When you say you, I presume you don't me, but my ex-wife."

"No Austin, I do mean you because the carer normally starts to feel the same symptoms as they Emphathise with the patient."

"Steph, you don't mind me calling you Stephen, do you?" Austin asked sharply.

Steph shook her head.

"What I am concerned about is my staff and as you have read in the newspapers nearly every family in the UK has at least one family member with some kind of mental health issue. I am concerned that my staff may try and avoid you."

"There are stages in recognizing bipolar. It starts with depression. Then manic episodes and then eventually hallucinations. It's a terrible illness," Stephanie stated calmly.

"I know I lived through two major episodes that made me realise that hell is on earth."

"Do you want to talk about?" she asked.

"No, not really as it was one of the darkest places in my life."

"Okay, take your time. I have asked your ex-wife to take her medication again. Here's the prescription."

"Can I take one?" requested Austin looking over the medication.

Stephanie smiled, "No, you need to be assessed first."

"I normally cook or write a book. I find that very therapeutic."

"And your ex-wife didn't?"

"She tried, her cooking was terrible and her writing was all against me."

"How did that make you feel?"

"Suicidal. Especially her cooking. Her meat was burnt, vegetables overcooked and potatoes undercooked. Cakes that stuck to the baking pan. I used to come early from work so that she didn't get a slot in the kitchen."

"Was she a kitchen jogger?"

"She hated the kitchen, washing machine, and dishwasher. Something to do with Women's Power and the teachings of the prophet. I thought she was just lazy," Austin finished with a shrug.

Stephanie hummed thoughtfully, "She was probably motivated by outside influence."

Austin scoffed, "I personally think she was just trying to avoid work, any kind of work."

"Did you ever ask her before the marriage if she suffered from any illnesses?"

"No, because marriage is a gamble, the more times one gets married, the better one gets at it. My motto is 'please me or leave me'."

"You mean a bit like God?" Stephanie asked wryly.

"Similar, more like a pharaoh."

In Egyptian society, religion held a central place in everyday life. One of the key roles of the king was to serve as an intermediary between the deities and the people. The king acted as a representative for the deities, serving in a dual capacity as both a civil and religious administrator. The king was the proprietor of all land in Egypt, established laws, collected taxes, and functioned as the military commander-in-chief. In religious matters, the king presided over ceremonies and determined the locations of new temples.

It was the king's responsibility to uphold Maat, representing cosmic order, balance, and justice. This duty included engaging in warfare when necessary to defend the country or launching attacks when believed to contribute to Maat, such as acquiring resources.

In the early days before the unification of Upper and Lower Egypt, the Deshret or "Red Crown" symbolized the kingdom of Lower Egypt, while the Hedjet, the "White Crown," was worn by the kings of Upper Egypt. Following the unification of both kingdoms, the Pschent, a combination of the red and white crowns, became the official crown of the pharaoh.

Over time, various headdresses were introduced during different dynasties, including the Khat, Nemes, Atef, Hemhem crown, and Khepresh. In certain depictions, a combination of these headdresses or crowns worn together was also portrayed.

The history and lore about the pharaohs makes one want to learn as much as possible since a lot of it is shrouded in mystery. As we navigate the annals of history, the pharaohs stand as silent witnesses to a civilization that left an indelible mark on the world. Their tombs whisper secrets, and their statues emanate a majestic presence, leaving us to ponder the depths of their wisdom and the mysteries that shroud their earthly reign.

4

Once Austin had compared himself to Pharaohs, it was harder for Stephanie to let that comment go. She wanted to get to know Austin's thoughts behind why he thought himself akin to Pharaohs.

The pharaoh served as a key authority in his state and acted as the necessary link connecting the gods and humanity. He oversaw the meticulous execution of temple rituals for the deities and assured the people of agricultural abundance, territorial defense, and fair dispensation of justice. Austin thought he was just like him, on a much smaller scale of course.

Within the sanctuaries, depictions of the sovereign are pervasive through wall scenes and statues. In this symbolic representation, the pharaoh is consistently portrayed as being on par with the gods. However, in religious discourse, he is merely depicted as a humble servant to the gods—a devoted servant who presents numerous offerings. This display of piety reflects the aspiration for a just reciprocation for his service.

Endowed with offerings, the gods are to benevolently unleash the forces of nature for the collective welfare of all Egyptians. As the sole individual permitted to engage in a discourse with the gods as equals, the Pharaoh assumes the role of the highest officiant, holding the foremost position among the country's priests. Moreover, the pharaonic action extends across all realms of collective activity, disregarding the division of powers. Every member of the administration operates solely in the name of the royal persona, acting through delegated authority.

Derived from the Pyramid Texts, the political endeavors of the ruler are encapsulated in a singular principle: "Bring Maat and repel Isfet," signifying the promotion of order and the repulsion of chaos. In the role of the caring patriarch for the people, the Pharaoh secures prosperity by invoking the gods to regulate the Nile's waters, opening granaries during times of famine, and ensuring an equitable distribution of arable land.

As the commander-in-chief of the armies, the pharaoh stands as the courageous defender of the borders. Just as Ra combats the serpent Apophis, the Egyptian king repels marauders from the desert, confronts invading forces, and quells internal uprisings.

The pharaoh consistently emerges as the solitary victor, whether standing resolute against a group of captives or launching arrows from his battle chariot. Holding the exclusive role of legislator, the laws and decrees he proclaims draw inspiration from divine wisdom. These regulations, stored in archives and overseen by the vizier, apply universally for the collective welfare and societal harmony.

The Pharaoh's daughter (Hebrew: בַּת־פַּרְעֹה, lit. 'daughter of Pharaoh') in the story of the finding of Moses in the biblical Book of Exodus is an important, albeit minor, figure in Abrahamic religions. While variations of her story exist, the general consensus among Jews, Christians, and Muslims is that she serves as the adoptive mother of the prophet Moses.

Muslims equate her with Asiya, the Great Royal Wife of the pharaoh. In both renditions, she rescues Moses from imminent danger posed by the Nile River and the Pharaoh. By ensuring Moses's well-being during his formative years, she played a crucial part in liberating the Hebrew slaves from Egyptian bondage, guiding them on their journey to the Promised Land, and contributing to the establishment of the Ten Commandments.

The story in the Jewish faith was that the daughter of Pharaoh came down to bathe at the river, and her maidens walked beside the river; she saw the basket among the reeds and sent her maid to fetch it. When she opened it she saw the child; and lo, the babe was crying. She took pity on him and said, "This is one of the Hebrews' children."

Then his sister said to Pharaoh's daughter, "Shall I go and call you a nurse from the Hebrew women to nurse the child for you?"

And Pharaoh's daughter said to her, "Go."

The girl went and summoned the child's mother. Pharaoh's daughter instructed her, "Take this child away, nurse him for me, and I will give you your wages."

The woman took the child and nursed him. As the child grew, she presented him to Pharaoh's daughter, who adopted him as her son and named him Moses, saying, "Because I drew him out of the water."

The Islamic version was that Pharaoh's daughter was not mentioned in any Islamic sources. In the Quranic narrative, Pharaoh's wife doesn't retrieve Moses from the Nile; instead, her servants do so. Upon learning of the boy's existence, Pharaoh aims to eliminate him, but his wife intervenes, leading Pharaoh to change his decision and spare the child's life. Similar to the Judeo-Christian account, Jochebed is summoned to Pharaoh's palace to serve as a wet nurse for Moses. Another wife of a different pharaoh during the exodus, named Asiya, acknowledges Moses' faith in God.

As per the Book of Exodus, Moses was born during a period when his people, the enslaved Israelites, were multiplying in number. This led to concerns for the Pharaoh, fearing that they might form alliances with Egypt's adversaries. In response, Moses' Hebrew mother, Jochebed, clandestinely concealed him when Pharaoh issued an order to eliminate all newborn Hebrew boys as a means to diminish the Israelite population.

Through Pharaoh's daughter (identified as Queen Bithia in the Midrash), the child was adopted as a foundling from the Nile and grew up with the Egyptian royal family.

After killing an Egyptian slave-master who was beating a Hebrew, Moses escaped to Midian by crossing the Red Sea. There, he encountered the Angel of the Lord speaking to him from a burning bush on Mount Horeb, which he identified as the Mountain of God. God sent Moses back to Egypt with the task of demanding the liberation of the Israelites from slavery.

Expressing a reluctance to speak eloquently, Moses was granted Aaron, his elder brother, as his spokesperson by God. Following the occurrence of the Ten Plagues, Moses led the Israelites in the Exodus out of Egypt, parting the Red Sea in the process. They eventually settled at Mount Sinai, where Moses received the Ten Commandments. After 40 years of wandering in the desert, Moses passed away at the age of 120 on Mount Nebo, overlooking the Promised Land.

In general, most scholars consider the biblical Moses to be a legendary figure, while acknowledging the potential existence of an individual resembling Moses in the 13th century BCE. Judaism has estimated Moses' lifespan to fall between 1391–1271 BCE; Jerome proposed 1592 BCE, and James Ussher suggested 1571 BCE as his birth year.

The Egyptian name "Moses" is mentioned in ancient Egyptian literature. According to the accounts of the Jewish historian Josephus, the ancient Egyptian historian Manetho wrote about a rebellious Egyptian priest named Osarseph, who adopted the name Moses and orchestrated a successful overthrow of the reigning pharaoh. Osarseph then governed Egypt for an extended period until the pharaoh reclaimed power and ousted Osarseph along with his followers.

"So, Austin do you consider yourself a Pharaoh or God?" Stephanie asked with a raise of her brow.

"Neither, I am Austin who prays to God and looks after the weak and poor people."

"You look after the weak and poor. Such as? How do you do that?"

"There's a couple I know. They are having marital problems, but they love each other. The husband is a lawyer and the wife is a homemaker. The wife was six months pregnant when they both came to see me. She was in deep depression and the husband was normal. I asked for them to give both sides of the story separately as otherwise they would both start arguing. The wife's story was that he was a loving husband both towards her and the children. However, he wanted to marry an old flame from his University days."

"And what was the husband's story?"

Austin smiled, "That he was still very much in love with this other woman, and instead of doing something unlawful, he would rather follow the law and marry this woman."

Stephanie nodded her head slowly, "And do you think that is wise?"

"In Islam, four marriages are allowed given that you are providing for all of them equally," Austin said.

"But still… it wouldn't be the same. Overall, he would start to spend less time with his first family than he did before. How is that fair for the first wife? And she is pregnant on top of that!" Stephanie asked with a raise of her brow.

Polygamy refers to the practice of having multiple spouses. In Islam, specifically termed as polygyny, only men can engage in polygamy. The subject of polygamy in the Quran has been a contentious issue, sparking ongoing debates. Many contend that polygamy is an unjust practice, alleging that some men pursue it for personal desires and sexual gratification.

The Quran addresses polygamy in several verses, including one found in the chapter titled Nisa (Women), which limits the number of wives to four.

In the pre-Islamic era, a practice existed where men would foster orphan girls and take possession of their belongings. Some of these men entered into marriages with these girls but failed to treat them justly and neglected to fulfill their bridal gift (mahr) obligations.

Verses in the Quran provide four key insights regarding polygamy. The Quran advises these men to consider marrying other women if they fear an inability to deal justly with the orphans. The Quran advises men to limit themselves to one wife if they are concerned about their ability to treat multiple wives fairly. An alternative option presented in the Quran for marrying orphans is to marry their slave-women. Throughout, the Quran consistently emphasizes the fair treatment of women. The term "qist" (justice) is mentioned at the beginning of the verse, while the term "'adl" (fair treatment) appears twice within the verse.

The terms "qist" and "'adl," both denoting justice, exhibit distinctions. "Qist" represents a higher level of justice, while "'adl" is a more commonplace form of justice. The usage of "qist" pertains to orphaned wives, whereas "'adl" is associated with ordinary wives. This differentiation arises from the heightened need for support that an orphaned girl experiences due to the loss of her father. Consequently, the man marrying her must exercise extra care to ensure fair treatment, respecting her honor and rights.

Before the arrival of Islam, individuals engaged in marriages with numerous women, and there was no imposed restriction on the number of wives one could have. In certain instances, the more influential and wealthy the men, the greater the number of their wives. Islam addressed this by asserting that polygamy is not a practice suitable for all men, introducing limitations to this custom, and halting the mistreatment of women, as many men practicing polygamy were found to treat their wives unjustly.

The Torah does not impose a prohibition on a man having multiple wives. Biblical figures such as Solomon, Ibrahim, David, and Jacob are notable examples of individuals in the Old Testament who had more than one wife. Numerous verses in the Old Testament provide guidance on the practice of polygamy. The verses address the practice of polygamy and outline specific guidelines to prevent mistreatment and ensure fairness among a man's wives. If a man chooses to take another wife, he must not diminish the provisions for his existing wife or wives in three key aspects: food, clothing, and marital rights. In terms of food, the husband is obligated to maintain the same standard and quantity of sustenance for each wife, preventing any disadvantage or neglect. Similarly, the provision of clothing must remain consistent for all wives, with no favouritism. Importantly, it is the husband's responsibility to uphold the marital rights of each wife, emphasizing the need for equitable treatment in intimate aspects of the relationship. Overall, the Old Testament establishes a framework for just and compassionate treatment within the context of polygamy, emphasizing the importance of fairness and consideration for the well-being of each wife in a multiple-spouse marriage.

While polygamy is mentioned in the Hebrew Bible (Old Testament), it is not a common practice among Jews today. Many Jewish communities abandoned polygamy in medieval times. In some cases, Jewish law allows a man to have more than one wife simultaneously, but this is subject to the approval of a Rabbinical court, and the practice is generally rare.

There are multiple verses in the New Testament based on which some are of the view that polygamy is allowed for men other than certain religious figures such as bishops and deacons. There are Christians who regard these verses as a ban on polygamy altogether. Some groups in the history of Christianity, such as certain early Christian sects and Mormons (in the 19th century), practiced polygamy, but these practices are not widely accepted today.

"So you think polygamy, sorry, polygyny, is alright?" Stephanie asked.

Austin shook his head, "If it is destabilizing your already happy marriage, then I don't believe you will be able to equalize the relationship you will have with the second wife and the one with your first wife. The problem here is not the second wife, but the fact that the husband is not marrying the second girl out of some kind of obligation or respect, he is doing that because his Nafs is weak. He was not able to remain unbothered by the appearance of his old flame which means there is a weakness in his faith. He should not be focusing or thinking of marrying, not before the husband has looked into himself and tried to strengthen his Nafs."

"And what is this Nafs?" Stephanie hummed as he wrote something down in her notebook.

"It is your inner soul, your inner self. It refers to a specific aspect of our self, encompassing desires, appetites, and what some may label as the ego. It encompasses various emotions like anger, passion, and lust. Some individuals may alternatively describe it as the carnal self or the carnal soul. It's crucial to note that the Nafs is distinct from the "ruh" or the soul. While the body and the Nafs constitute the physical aspects of our being, God has also endowed us with an inner or spiritual element, known as our ruh. The Nafs is integral to our physical self, though it is not a part of our physical body per se."

Stephanie folded her hands and leaned back in her chair, "And you helped this couple by giving this advice? That the husband should have more control over himself."

Austin nodded, "But I also told the wife to bring back the things they used to do at the start. Having children can be a lot, but still, a marriage requires attention, care, and love. If you are not putting all of these things into a bond, it is meant to weaken."

"So you told them both to try a little bit harder to get back to what they had before they were distracted by… life."

"I tried my best to help them out," Austin shrugged, "Marriage is a big deal and destroying one just so you could have another is not the most wisest decision."

"And how is this couple doing these days?" Stephanie asked with a raise of her brow.

"Well," Austin drawled, "They must be doing better because they haven't come cursing at me."

And they both burst out into laughter.

5

Qayamat held significant importance in Islam, marking the day when, following death, individuals would face judgment. Those who adhered to Allah's laws (halal) and were considered righteous would be destined for heaven (Jannat), while those who transgressed Allah's laws (haram) would face hell (Jahannum). Michelangelo depicted this concept on the walls of the Sistine Chapel in Rome.

While interpretations of what the Quran and hadeeth say about the end times are 'diverse and complex,' the signs of Judgment Day's arrival include disruptions in the order of both human morality and the natural world. Additionally, the appearance of the savior(s) Mahdi and Jesus 'is seen to represent the ultimate victory of the Ummah of Islam in some senses.'

Piety will decline with the prevalence of music, wine drinking, usury, homosexuality, disobedience by wives, and fornication, leading to the destruction of the earth. However, during this era, ʿĪsā (Jesus) and the Mahdi will triumph over the Antichrist figure al-Dajjāl, and Allah will eliminate the monstrous Gog and Magog, thereby liberating the world from injustice and restoring sharia.

The signs have been categorized into minor and major by commentators. Various ḥadīth collections report them, and they are elucidated in commentaries by numerous medieval Muslim scholars, including al-Ghazali, Ibn Kathir, and Muhammad al-Bukhari, among others. Islamic apocalyptic literature that describes Armageddon (or fitna) is commonly referred to as Al-Malhama Al-Kubra (The Great Epic).

Austin cherished the world, especially the Buxton mountains leading into Macclesfield, always grateful for Allah's creation of such a beautiful place. Then the first man, Adam, came who wondered alone.

According to the creation myth of the Abrahamic religions, Adam and Eve held the roles of the first man and woman. Their significance lies in the belief that humanity constitutes a single family, all descended from this initial pair of ancestors. Additionally, they form the foundation for doctrines such as the fall of man and original sin, which are significant tenets in Christianity but not shared in Judaism or Islam.

In the Book of Genesis within the Hebrew Bible, specifically chapters one through five, two creation narratives present distinct perspectives. In the initial narrative, Adam and Eve remain unnamed. Instead, humankind is created in the image of God and given the directive to multiply, acting as stewards over all of God's creations.

In the second narrative, God forms Adam from dust and places him in the Garden of Eden. Adam is granted the freedom to eat from all the trees in the garden, except for the tree of the knowledge of good and evil.

Subsequently, Eve is created from one of Adam's ribs to serve as his companion. At this point, they are innocent and unashamed of their nakedness. However, a serpent persuades Eve to eat fruit from the forbidden tree, and she, in turn, shares it with Adam.

These actions not only bestow upon them additional knowledge but also grant them the ability to evoke negative and destructive concepts, such as shame and evil. Subsequently, God imposes curses on the serpent and the ground. God prophetically outlines the consequences of disobedience for the woman and the man. Finally, God banishes them from the Garden of Eden.

During one of their session, Austin asked Stephanie who had previously mentioned that she was an atheist, "Where does the sun rise from?"

Stephanie raised a brow at him and answered, "East of course."

Austin nodded, "Good, and what's the function of our good old sun?"

"Daylight," Stephanie immediately answered.

"And?" Austin asked her to elaborate.

Stephanie shrugged, "Don't know," after a bit of thinking she added, "Make plants grow?"

Austin hummed, "Of course," then asked again, "And who eats plants?"

Stephanie answered, "Animals?"

Austin shrugged as he told her, "Humans need food, meat and rain. So the sun is very powerful and was created first by Allah."

Further, we note that the great lights to rule the day and night are placed in the firmament (Gen 1:14); now, according to Gen 1:6, the firmament is the space (sky) between the water below (rivers, seas, lakes, etc) and the waters above (clouds or the source of rain, hail & snow, etc)."

When Steph used to go to sites, Austin used to ring ahead to the site manager that she was on her way. The site manager would then go around the site to let everyone know. Suddenly all the men would hide in large concrete pipes, in toilets, and behind piles of mud.

Steph had a plan to marry a rich man. She was pretty, a brunette with a slight lisp. After recently being diagnosed with vertigo, she sometimes felt dizzy. She sometimes worked all day and night to pay her bills, and there never was enough left for her to find the rich man when she was a student with one son.

If it was not sad, then it was just too bad. If she had found a rich man as was her plan, she wouldn't have to work at all. She would just fool around and make sure her son grew nice and tall. But would a wealthy have enough Gaul? It was Austin's world where he had millions from lucrative contracts. He specifically tendered for energy projects that included a thirty percent markup instead of the normal ten percent in construction.

However, Steph was concerned about her son and with all the wars going on in the world she had asked Austin, "How long do you think it will be before the Palestinians have justification?"

Austin was quick to answer, "Until fossil fuel is around there will be always some kind of tension in the world, whether it's Palestine, Syria, Iraq, or Iran. Either adopt Americans or let them rule."

The only country that beat the Western domination was Afghanistan. Afghanistan has over 1,400 mineral fields, containing barite, chromite, coal, copper, gold, iron ore, lead, natural gas, petroleum, precious and semi-precious stones, salt, sulfur, lithium, talc, and zinc, among many other minerals. Gemstones include high-quality emeralds, lapis lazuli, red garnet, and ruby.

As per a collaborative study conducted by The Pentagon and the United States Geological Survey, Afghanistan possessed an estimated US$1 trillion worth of untapped minerals. The conflict in Afghanistan was not solely directed against terrorists but was also aimed at gaining access to these mineral surveys.

The strategic importance of Afghanistan in terms of energy was derived from its geographical location, serving as a crucial transit route for the export of oil, natural gas, and electricity from Central Asia to South Asia and the Arabian Sea. This potential included the development of the Trans-Afghanistan Pipeline gas pipeline.

Approximately forty million years ago, a monumental collision between the tectonic plates of India-Europe, Asia, and Africa occurred, resulting in significant upheaval. This geological event gave rise to the towering mountainous region that encompasses present-day Afghanistan. The country's abundant resources position it as one of the most lucrative mining regions globally.

In a general sense, Americans, often characterized as assertive and driven by self-interest, have exerted considerable efforts to assert control over Afghanistan, beginning with confrontations against Russia in the 1990s. Similar tendencies were observed in Palestine, where terrorists aimed to hinder the Western world's access to natural resources. Consequently, the conflict was not merely against terrorists but rather a strategic pursuit to secure access to these valuable resources.

When Austin shared this bit with Steph, she said, "So in reality there are no terrorists."

"No, just normal soldiers defending their sovereignty against the western world. Not many people know that," Austin added.

"What about young girls running off to Syria?" Steph asked.

"Teenage trauma, hormones, family issues. Don't girls run off to London? Don't some girls want to marry a soldier or a fireman?"

"I did marry a soldier," Steph added with a sardonic chuckle.

"It's every parent's worst nightmare—you go to check on your child in the middle of the night, and she's not there. Your heart starts pounding and you fly into panic mode, calling her friends, your relatives, and the police."

Steph hummed thoughtfully, then asked, "So did your daughter run away?"

"My nieces," Austin replied. He continued, "Don't forget, running away is like any action. In order to do it you need three things: the ability, the willingness, and the opportunity. And let's face it, kids have the opportunity and ability to run every day—so all it really takes is the willingness to do it. That willingness can develop for a variety of reasons. It could be a stressful situation your child is under, a fear of getting consequences for something they did, a form of power struggle, not wanting to go to school, or a substance abuse problem."

"Isn't it to do with boyfriends?" Steph mused.

"That real factor is that kids often idealize running away and develop a romanticized view of life on the streets. In reality, it's awful: you're cold, you're hungry and it's dangerous, but adolescents often see it as an adventure or the key to freedom, where 'No one is going to tell me what to do.'"

Steph nodded in agreement as Austin continued, "Many kids run away because of drug and alcohol abuse. When teens and pre-teens get involved in substance abuse, they may leave home to hide it so their parents don't find out. These kids are often using a lot more than their parents know; they want to use more freely and openly, so they run away."

"What about fear and anxiety?" She asked hoping that her child wouldn't run away.

"In addition to fear or anger, feelings of failure can also cause kids to leave home. Some children run away because it's easier to live on their own than to live in a critical home. I remember being 15 years old and living in a hallway in a block of flats in winter. I didn't miss home at all because I felt like such a failure there. Sadly, kids with behavior management problems or learning disabilities often get tired of the feeling that they just can't get it right; it's easier for them to run than to fix the problem. Often, they don't know that what they're facing can be dealt with using other strategies," Austin elaborated.

Then Steph stepped in to say, "In my opinion, the main reason why kids run away is because they don't have good problem-solving skills. Running away is an "either/or" kind of solution; it's a product of black-and-white thinking. Kids run away because they don't want to face something, and that includes emotions they don't want to deal with. The adolescent who runs away has run out of problem-solving skills. And leaving home—along with everything that is overwhelming them—seems to solve their immediate problems."

Austin listened to her quietly, then asked, "Do you know about the warning signs?"

Steph shrugged, "I think so."

"Unfortunately, there are no real hard-and-fast signs that indicate your child is about to run away. Certainly, you can look for secretive behavior, the hoarding of money, and things of value disappearing around the house. If you ever notice this happening, don't turn a blind eye: trust your gut. You probably already know that something is up, whether it's substance abuse or your child's desire to leave home."

"So, how did you manage your niece?" she asked then.

"It was one of the hardest things I did. Bringing separated parents and making them responsible. All parents should have a system where they check in with their kids frequently. Just stop and ask, 'How's it going? Anything you want help with? You can say this two or three times in one day; go by their room and knock on the door. That way you're constantly giving your child hypodermic interest and affection. You're saying, 'I'm interested in you, I care.' This is a skill that parents can build; it doesn't always come naturally. I understand that parents who have worked all day come home and they're tired. My wife and I were both social workers and when we came home, the last thing we wanted to do was talk some more. But we trained ourselves to do that so our son would know we were interested and that we cared. You never lose when you show that to a child."

Both Steph and Austin walked back to the site office which was located on the upper level of a set of four 32-foot temporary offices. Austin made Steph and himself a cup of coffee. He looked around whilst standing up. "What do you think of the office setup?" he asked.

"It looks good, more or less the same surroundings as a normal office," Steph replied with a smile.

"Why? You may ask. The reason is the people on site make money for the company and they shouldn't have to be treated any less than a person in the office. Furthermore, the Prophet Muhammad (PBUH) emphasized the importance of paying employees on time and treating them with kindness and respect. He said, "Give the worker his wages before his sweat dries." This hadith emphasizes the importance of paying employees promptly and not delaying their wages."

"Not many employers do that," Steph commented.

"I do because it's good for their mental health and family life."

"Before they actually do the work?"

"Yes, but I don't keep anyone who doesn't work hard as The Holy Prophet. He always insisted on working hard. He is reported to have said: One who works is the friend of Allah, and one who does not work is considered by Allah, to be His enemy."

Austin's company had gone from strength to strength and he had made his money through working hard himself.

"Let me re-iterate. At the time of judgment day. Allah will ask two things. First what was my intention and second, my method of achieving my intention. My method is the Hadeeth. Anyone can Google the specific Hadeeth," Austin added.

"So, if everyone follows the two stage process everyone will be a winner?" Steph asked with intrigue.

"Exactly, no poverty, no wars, and certainly no fornication. Let me give you an example," Austin said as he typed into Google search Engine. "There you are 'Fornification.' It's a wrong intent to be adulterous as it affects a lot of families."

"My ex-boyfriend left me for another woman," Steph shared.

"My ex-wife left me for another man."

"Sharia law tries to enforce sexual morality to the core and anyone who is found guilty of fornication is punished with one hundred lashes and a married Muslim who is found guilty of adultery may be stoned by a group of Muslim believers until that person dies to send a clear warning to wannabe adulterers. It still happens in many places in the world," Austin explained.

"Do you think that is right?" Steph inquired.

"What I believe or not believe doesn't really matter. It's what the Hadeeth believes."

"That's a bit harsh isn't it?" Steph mused.

"Isn't it harsh on your son that his father no longer lives with his mother?" Austin countered.

Steph admitted, “He has gone very quiet after the divorce, my ex does come around, but it’s not the same thing.”

“So in Sharia law, a man is allowed to marry four times so he keeps in touch with his children and still shares the bed with his wife. They should all live in one house and kids play together.”

“I don’t think I could do that,” Steph added.

“No one is asking you to,” Austin added, then continued, “but you have to look at it from every angle. The father falls out with in over a family dispute, rather than going out to some strange woman, he goes to the best wife he has for comfort. Probably stays the night with her and she advises him from the point of the woman. So the husband returns to his other wife and patches up the family dispute. Everything is done what I call In-house.”

“If there was no ‘best wife?’”

“Then there is always the marriage guidance. Who obviously need to understand the issues, analyze and recommend actions. This will not only take another man or woman away from their family life but will cost money. Obviously, there are exceptions,” Austin shrugged.

“Exceptions?” Steph asked, quirking a brow.

“Yes, an Arab friend fell out with all four wives and had to divorce them because he fell in love with a prostitute. Which is not allowed in Shariah law.”

“So is it the woman’s job to keep the straight and narrow?”

“Exactly, Eve didn’t and look at the mess the world is in,” Austin stated.

"So do you believe in Sharia Law or British Law?" Steph asked after a moment of silence,

"I believe in a mixture of the two, especially the bit about the four wives," Austin admitted.

Steph laughed out loud.

Austin continued despite that, "I wish Rihanna was that accepting, in fact, she told me that if I went with another woman, she would stab me whilst I was sleeping, cut me in small pieces, and bury me under a concrete foundation. She has mellowed a bit though. I can now stare, drool, and dance, but can touch but not grope. A sort of compromise."

Steph leaned back in her chair thoughtfully, then asked, "What does the Hadeeth say about that?"

"It's what is called a broken heart syndrome. British Heart Foundation is funding the syndrome and found that whether you've had a breakup, lost someone you love, or experienced any extremely upsetting or stressful event, it could affect you. It's called Takotsubo."

In a groundbreaking study funded by the British Heart Foundation, researchers have made a concerning discovery about the treatments administered to individuals diagnosed with broken heart syndrome.

The University of Aberdeen Cardiology and Cardiovascular Research Unit found that patients with broken heart syndrome receive the same medication as those who have had a heart attack, based on their analysis of data from 3,720 individuals over a decade. Although this treatment approach proved effective for heart attack survivors, it did not enhance the survival rate of those with Takotsubo.

Participants experiencing broken heart syndrome were found to have a higher likelihood of mortality compared to the general population. Their susceptibility to death was similar to that of patients who had experienced a 'true' heart attack, and they exhibited an increased vulnerability to the development of heart conditions.

Here's a comprehensive guide to the "devastating illness," featuring insights from experts and a survivor who experienced it following a significant loss. This condition arises in response to distressing events, such as the death of a family member, the termination of a relationship, or illness, where distress signals travel from the brain to the heart.

However, knowledge is expanding, and there is emerging evidence suggesting that it can also be triggered by other factors, including physical trauma or even without a specific incident.

Steph listened as he explained about the disease, "Takotsubo cardiomyopathy happens when one of the heart's chambers, the left ventricle, suddenly balloons and weakens. The heart then can't pump blood around the body as before and the extra stress leads to heart failure. It can develop at any age, and typically affects more women than men."

Symptoms can appear like a heart attack, including shortness of breath and chest pain.

"But Takotsubo cardiomyopathy is a different condition entirely and unlike a heart attack, patients don't suffer from a blockage of the arteries that supply the heart with blood," Austin added.

That was how their session that day came to an end. Talking with Steph was always productive and Austin enjoyed imparting the knowledge he had gained over the years of working.

"Nice session today, Austin," Steph said, shaking his hand.

Austin bowed his head and returned to work.

X

It was the year 2038.

Rihanna was inside of the United Nations Building having a conversation about her husband, Austin.

"My new zannusi washing machine actually talks to me in the morning whereas my useless husband just walks on by in his pajamas."

"Why don't you just get rid of him?" one of her acquaintances asked.

Rihanna shrugged, "I'll have to give him alimony."

"It might be easier to get him knocked off."

Rihanna crossed one leg over the other as she thought about her life with Austin. "I read somewhere that Researchers explained men with breadwinner wives or partners are likely to endure "stigma and social sanctions" such as "gossiping, ridicule, and judgment" for not abiding by stereotypes of masculinity."

Her friend scoffed, "I find my husband gossiping a lot with other men. It seems to be like they are talking about the end of the world and the Coercion Act of Law 2021."

"I told Austin that it's an outdated law and doesn't really apply to men," said Rihanna.

"How old is Austin now?"

"Seventy-eight this coming July."

"Only six weeks away?"

"We don't celebrate his birthday anymore. He doesn't like all the fuss. He said that he is fed up with birthday cakes and blowing candles. He is suffering from bronchitis, but still does the odd jobs around the mansion."

"He can't be that busy surely."

"He works on mathematical models and predictions when the world would end."

"Oh, that Malarkey."

"Yeah, that old chestnut," Rihanna added as she laughed out loud.

Her friend raised a brow, "Are you sure he's not going senile?"

"No, I had him checked out and the doctors say he's fine. He's however moving slowly and takes his time doing the odd jobs. He complains about his knees and breathing when bending down and struggles to prostate when praying to his Allah. Sometimes I hear him crying loudly when prostrating as if he is asking for forgiveness from the whole world. Then when he gets up he is smiling."

They both chuckled as her friend added, "Definitely going senile."

Limited research has delved into the motivations behind individuals making apocalyptic forecasts. Throughout history, such predictions have often served various purposes, including diverting attention away from pressing issues such as poverty and warfare, advancing political agendas, and fostering animosity towards specific groups. For instance, medieval Christian apocalyptic predictions frequently centered on themes of antisemitism, while depictions by French and Lutheran groups often featured

English and Catholic adversaries, respectively. Psychologists suggest several potential reasons for contemporary belief in apocalyptic prophecies, including simplifying complex global threats into a single identifiable cause, a fundamental human fascination with fear, personal characteristics like paranoia and feelings of powerlessness, and a modern cultural fascination with end-times narratives popularized in contemporary fiction.

The widespread influence of Abrahamic religions across modern history is believed to have fostered a cultural inclination toward anticipating a future markedly different from the present. This cultural backdrop is often cited as a contributing factor to the surge in popularity of secular predictions, such as the 2012 phenomenon, while still retaining the age-old motif that a formidable force will herald the demise of humanity.

The next prediction was forecasted by Said Nursi, a Sunni Muslim theologian, author of the Risale-i Nur, and founder of the Nur movement, who wrote in a letter to one of his students (the 21st in the so-called Kastamonu Appendix) that by applying numerology to a hadith he had arrived at a date of 1545 for the arrival of doomsday. 1545 in the Hijri calendar would be 2122; in the Rumi calendar, it would be 2129. Nursî added that this was not a definite prediction, as "nobody knows the time of doom in a strict manner".

These predictions have been way out, apparently, there's one predicted by Talmud, an orthodox Jew. As outlined in mainstream Orthodox Judaism's interpretation of the Talmud, the Messiah is expected to arrive within a few years of the creation of Adam, with the potential for the world's destruction occurring approximately 1000 years later. By this calculation, the period of desolation would commence around 2239 and conclude with the period of complete desolation around 3239.

Rihanna sighed, "Austin's predicting it as mid 2052. He will be 108," she shook her head, "That's it then. It's all about me, me, me with him. If he has to die he wants the whole world to die with him."

"Is that why he cries when prostrating?"

"I think he's a bit of a crybaby. Probably thinks if he suffers the whole world should suffer with him."

"Is he that bad?" her friend asked.

Rihanna nodded, "Oh yeah, but in the last five years he has been getting up early and I don't really know what he does, but in the shed, he has developed a model of a volcano set up our old marble table. He won't tell me what it is. Below the table, there are seven trumpets, pointing towards an upside volcano model. He's burnt the dinner twice in the last few days and said he forgets to turn the oven off."

"Must be difficult living with someone who burns dinner for a lady who works her stockings off."

"I know I get to the mansion sometimes really late after the pubs close because I have late meetings in the bar and what do I get?"

"Excuses, excuses, and more excuses."

"Exactly, the men think that the world revolves around them. I have to tell Austin that the world revolves around me as head of the United Nations."

Austin had read somewhere that, "Upon the sound of the first trumpet, hail and fire mingled with blood is thrown to Earth, burning up a third of the trees on the planet, and all green grass".

With the sound of the second trumpet, something described as "a great mountain burning with fire" plunges into the sea and turns a third of the ocean to blood. Soon after, a third of all sea life and a third of all ships will be destroyed.

Upon the sounding of the third trumpet, a colossal star named Wormwood descends to Earth, contaminating a third of its freshwater sources, including rivers and springs, causing many to perish due to its bitter taste.

Subsequent to the sounding of the fourth trumpet, a third of the luminance emitted by the Sun, moon, and stars dims as these celestial bodies are "struck," resulting in complete darkness for one-third of the day, extending into the night hours. This marks the final trumpet before the onset of the three woes, also referred to as the fifth, sixth, and seventh trumpets.

The fifth trumpet heralds the commencement of the "first woe" among the three. Preceding the sounding of this trumpet, an angel (referred to as an eagle in certain translations) appears and issues a warning: "Woe, woe, woe to those who dwell on the earth, because of the remaining blasts of the trumpet of the three angels who are about to sound."

The fifth trumpet initiates the descent of a personified star from heaven, bestowed with the key to the bottomless pit. Upon unlocking it, smoke billows forth, obscuring the air and eclipsing sunlight. From within this smoke emerge locusts, resembling warhorses with scorpion tails, possessing human faces adorned with lion-like teeth. They possess lengthy hair and soar with wings akin to locusts. Adorned with golden crowns and armored in iron breastplates, they serve under the command of their king, Abaddon, tasked with tormenting those lacking the seal of God on their foreheads, utilizing their scorpion-like tails. It is explicitly stated that they are forbidden from causing death during the five-month period of torment.

Austin tried to sequence the blowing of the trumpets and just above the inverted volcano he suspended a dosimeter. On the wall of the shed, there was a Sound graph. The model resembled the Grindsvik volcano in Iceland, which has maintained activity for centuries and is located near the North Pole. In 2023, it exhibited renewed activity, characterized by the emergence of fissures encircling its base approximately three miles below ground level. This phenomenon resembled reflective cracking outlining the base at a depth of three miles.

Austin heard the BBC news and the Volcanic Expert didn't even consider the fissures, but seemed chirpy and talking about having drinks after the field visits with other specialists and joking that they would never see the final eruption in her lifetime and if there was nothing to worry about.

Rihanna then spoke at the meeting once every delegate settled down after the initial meeting in the bar. She started quite casually, leaning back slightly in her chair. "Ladies, sorry there are no gentlemen here since the UN appointed an all-women delegation as head of states for the last decade, everything seems to be in order. The working male population has dropped dramatically, not because women are more efficient, can multi-task, and are better looking, but because men are born lazy and useless. The Coercion Act 2021 was overturned by myself as the women turned the tables on the stupid men. Now we can say whatever we want without any legal repercussions."

The delegates stood up and clapped and some women whistled. Then Rihanna started talking again, "The population has surpassed ten billion, ladies and ladies and just under five billion are men."

She paused for a second and passed a look around the room. "But, I had a dream, and now I have a plan to reduce the population. This plan I am proposing will not only reduce the population but will reduce food prices by twenty-five percent around the world," she said with a nod.

There were further claps but this time there was no standing ovation. Rihanna moved on and started the PowerPoint presentation.

"First slide please," she muttered.

The first slide showed a graph of population growth over the last 50 years. It indicated that in the year 2025, the population was eight point six billion.

She pointed at the screen as she talked, "There you have it we introduced the AI husband in 2031 and the rate of growth has decreased dramatically, but it will not reduce by 2083 as everywoman cannot afford an AI husband. My job is to get cheaper AI into every home and for men to start making them. The cost of electricity, cost of land, and cost of batteries have all shot up."

She tilted her head to the side, "Next slide please," Rihanna took a deep breath then continued, "Cost of land has doubled in the last decade, cost of raw materials have trebled, labour costs have increased four-fold. I am not playing or mincing words here, but are facts made only possible by continuous wars declared by men, proving their macho factor over one another."

This went on until the end of the PowerPoint presentation.

"Next slide, please," she said again. "This was my dream, where men were sent to Mars to reduce the population, we control their food, water, and air. In fact, we become their goddesses not their whores. They don't control us, we control them."

Suddenly everyone started clapping to a standing ovation.

"Next slide please!"

"A world without men will be a peaceful place, a better place and we can thrive so that our children live in peace."

"Next slide Please."

"So in the next five years, I have a plan to send all men over the age of fifty to Mars, including my husband Austin, but before I do that I need to ensure all the money, property, and his classic cars collection is handed over to me."

All the delegates stood up again and clapped. Rihanna bowed and walked off the podium to a standing ovation.

***

The colonization or settlement of Mars refers to the conceptual human migration and establishment of a long-term human presence on the planet. This idea has captured the attention of both public space agencies and private corporations and has been a prominent theme in science fiction literature, film, and art. Various organizations have put forth plans for human missions to Mars, which would represent the initial phase of any colonization endeavor.

However, to date, no human has landed on the planet, and there have been no return missions. Nevertheless, landers and rovers have effectively conducted exploration missions on the Martian surface, providing valuable data about the environmental conditions on the planet.

The primary distinction lies in gravity, with individuals experiencing approximately one-third of Earth's gravitational force. This gravitational variance may have adverse effects on human health, including the weakening of bones and muscles, as well as an increased risk of osteoporosis and cardiovascular issues. Astronauts aboard the International Space Station currently undergo rotations in zero gravity for six months, a duration comparable to a one-way journey to Mars.

This allows researchers to gain insights into the physical condition astronauts may face upon reaching Mars. Once on the Martian surface, gravity is only 38% of that on Earth, and microgravity influences various bodily systems, including cardiovascular, musculoskeletal, and neurovestibular (central nervous) systems. The cardiovascular effects of microgravity are multifaceted and intricate.

On Earth, approximately 70% of the blood in the body is situated below the heart, but in microgravity environments, this distribution changes due to the absence of gravitational force pulling the blood downward. This alteration can lead to several adverse effects.

Upon entering microgravity, blood pressure in the lower body and legs experiences a significant decrease, resulting in muscle and bone mass loss and subsequent weakness in the legs. Astronauts often exhibit symptoms such as facial puffiness and what is colloquially termed "chicken legs syndrome."

Upon re-entry to Earth after spending time in space, blood samples have shown a 17% reduction in plasma volume, contributing to decreased secretion of erythropoietin. Prolonged exposure to microgravity also affects the skeletal system, leading to demineralization and muscle atrophy, which are vital for maintaining posture.

During the re-acclimation phase, astronauts commonly experience symptoms like cold sweats, nausea, vomiting, and motion sickness, along with feelings of disorientation. Given that journeys to and from Mars typically last around six months, similar to the average duration spent at the International Space Station (ISS), the reduced gravity on Mars (approximately 38% of Earth's surface gravity) would exacerbate these health concerns. Upon returning to Earth, recovering from bone loss and muscle atrophy is a protracted process, and the effects of microgravity may persist indefinitely without full reversal.

Rihanna went back to the bar and ordered a martini. A few other delegates gathered around. Then a lady in a husky voice said, "Darling, that was really good." Then she kissed Rihanna on the lips.

Rihanna's lips curled up, "Thanks, darling, Cider?"

"Of course," the lady drawled, "Get me drunk and take advantage of me. I was actually turned on by your passion to get rid of men."

Rihanna winked, "And we shall. We don't need them anymore, we won't have to see them ever."

Both women started to laugh loudly. This attracted the attention of a young lady, who approached them and said, "Glad to see someone happy. What are some signs I might be a lesbian? Is there a test to see if I am a lesbian or not? When I question about my sexuality and wonder if I am a lesbian or not, I may be hoping there are certain signs that may help me figure it out."

"The best test is when watching a movie, are your eyes drawn to the women or to the men?"

"Both," the young lady replied.

"You're LBGTQ compliant then, you will have no issue in living in the new world order. The surprised you're not wearing the flag."

Gilbert Baker, a gay artist, deliberately chose the rainbow to symbolize the LGBTQ community as he sought to convey a message of pride and diversity through a natural symbol. He believed the rainbow was an ideal representation due to its presence in nature.

In the late 1970s, Harvey Milk, an openly gay official in the United States, approached Gilbert Baker to create a symbol for the LGBTQ community. In 1978, the first LGBTQ flags were crafted, featuring hot pink, turquoise, and indigo, comprising eight colors. However, for mass production efficiency, pink and turquoise were eliminated, and indigo was substituted with blue. Consequently, the current LGBTQ flag consists of six colors: red, orange, yellow, green, blue, and violet, each carrying significant symbolism.

"So, if you change your mind about the LBGTQ we will still have men, but young men still on earth so we as women can brainwash them into thinking like women. We think that it's the older generation that is a major huddle against our quest to rule the world, that includes Austin. He keeps going on Prophet Lut from Sodom, I thought he was talking about a bouncer in a nightclub," Rihanna regaled with a sigh.

"Don't you mean Lot? As in the Old Testament?" the lady asked.

Rihanna shrugged, "Probably, I have no idea what he goes on about half the time."

"I did read about Sodom and Gommarah, which I thought was quite interesting," the lady replied with a hum.

"Genesis 13:12 and 19:29 covers it specifically."

"Wasn't that Phil Collins Group?"

"Yes and what a great drummer he was."

"Their album Genesis to Revelation was excellent, but was sold in the religious section of the record stores and was a flop."

"So what was Genesis?"

"It was a timeline of when God created the heavens and earth. In the beginning, God created the heaven and the earth. And the earth was without form and void, and darkness was upon the face of the deep. And the Spirit of God moved upon the face of the waters. And God said, Let there be light: and there was light."

"Austin said that Moses wrote the first five books of Genesis."

"It is covered both in the Torah and the Old Testament. Its first word is 'Bereshit' the first chapter was written on an egg. On the first day there was light, second day God separated the waters and the land. On the third day there was rain and vegetation appeared on the land. On the fourth day, God sets the light so can distinguish between day and night. On the fifth day, fish and birds appeared and were asked to multiply. On the sixth day, humans were created to inhabit the earth and asked to multiply. God declared his creation as 'very good."

"And on the seventh day?" the lady asked, leaning forward in intrigue.

"God rested, calling it a holy day."

"It was in the garden of Eden, that it went tits up."

"God forbade humans not to eat from the forbidden tree but can eat from any other tree in the garden. It was the tree of knowledge of good and evil, if the man ate it, he would surely die."

Next in the evolutionary timeline is Ardipithecus, the earliest known genus in the human lineage and believed to be the probable ancestor of Australopithecus, a closely related group often regarded as ancestral to modern humans. Ardipithecus existed between 5.8 million and 4.4 million years ago and is primarily known from the remains of a partial female skeleton known as Ardi.

Notably, Ardi's braincase was similar in size to that of a chimpanzee, and she possessed long arms and fingers, as well as opposable great toes, although lacking large sharpened canine teeth typical of apes. Ardi's pelvis and foot exhibited more similarities with later members of the human lineage rather than with apes, leading researchers to conclude that she was likely capable of walking, despite presumably spending a considerable amount of time in arboreal environments.

These early primates may have been among the first to primarily navigate their surroundings by walking upright, marking a significant development in the early stages of human evolution. However, it's probable that bipedalism emerged earlier in species such as Sahelanthropus tchadensis (existing 7.2–6.8 million years ago), Orrorin tugenensis (approximately 6 million years ago), or Ardipithecus (living 5.8–4.4 million years ago).

Around 4.4 million years ago in East Africa, australopithecines displayed a blend of human-like and ape-like characteristics. Possessing elongated arms and curved fingers suited for tree-dwelling, their leg length was shorter compared to contemporary humans. While incapable of speech, their brains were slightly larger than those of chimpanzees. Notably, in 1974, paleontologist Donald C. Johanson discovered the well-preserved skeleton of a young Australopithecus afarensis in Hadar, Ethiopia, whom he named Lucy. Lucy remains one of the most renowned fossils ever discovered.

Rihanna suddenly perked up, "Lucy? Austin used to call me that, when we slept together, I thought that was a bit on the side."

"It could be that there two tribes were formed one from Prophet Seth and the other one from Cain. Supposedly it was Cain who murdered Zable and buried him, therefore a ritual that all Jews, Christians, and Muslims follow. However, Cain went against God's commands and raised a version of polygamy. In time, the Cain gene has been dominant on Earth through Satan.

Austin questioned whether that is the reason why idolism still exists as money is made out of selling idols. The goddess of wealth was the best-selling idol, ironically making the seller very rich, similar to pyramid selling. God's command was not to unnecessarily spend money on items not needed for survival and yet the generation of Cain went over and above the commandments of God. No wonder Austin thought that Moses was mad at the Israelites as they danced around the golden calf, it reminded him of Cain who murdered Able, thus starting a mother of all wars through Satan.

After Cain murdered Able, he was jealous that God accepted Able's sacrifice and not his. Cain was the firstborn of Adam and Eve, having murdered Able, God punished him to a life of wandering.

In the Qur'an, Abel and Cain are referred to as Hābīl (هابيل) and Qābīl (قابيل) respectively. The narrative in the Qur'an closely mirrors that found in the Hebrew Bible: Both brothers were instructed to present offerings to God individually; God favored Abel's sacrifice over Cain's; consumed by envy, Cain murdered Abel, marking the first instance of homicide on Earth. Within Islam, the tale of Cain and Abel serves as a warning against the grave sin of murder, emphasizing the sanctity of human life.

X – 1

Children are blessings from Allah, undoubtedly bestowed upon us as invaluable treasures. Each child is a distinct individual deserving of utmost respect and dignity, which underscores our belief in the sanctity of life as Muslims. It is incumbent upon us to treat children with kindness, ensuring they receive quality care and opportunities to flourish. Allah regards all children as precious and deserving of love, nurturing, and dignified care, fostering their holistic development. The Islamic faith underscores the importance of respecting and honoring children.

A child is a divine gift from Allah, embodying innocence and beauty. In Islam, it is strictly forbidden to address children in anger. It is imperative to always show kindness and refrain from speaking harshly to them. Both the Holy Quran and hadiths caution against expressing anger towards children. Parents bear the duty to cherish, nurture, and safeguard their children, as exemplified by the teachings of Prophet Muhammad, peace be upon him.

As children are manifestations of Allah's mercy upon us, Islam teaches us to treat them with affection, respect, and patience. Our revered Prophet Muhammad, peace be upon him, exemplified this love and patience in his interactions with children, serving as a model for us to emulate. Therefore, it is incumbent upon us to follow in the footsteps of our beloved Prophet and uphold the fear of Allah in our hearts regarding the fundamental rights of children.

Equality holds significant importance in Islam, particularly when it comes to children, where it assumes utmost significance. Favoring one child over another is deemed inappropriate. In Islam, both males and females are regarded as equally precious. Parents are entrusted with specific obligations towards their children, encompassing providing shelter, sustenance, clothing, education, guidance, and care.

By demonstrating compassion towards others, we can earn the mercy of Allah. Charity stands as one of the five pillars of Islam, playing a pivotal role in fostering a compassionate society where individuals prioritize the well-being of others alongside their own and their families.

Muslims who engage in acts of charity perceive it as their obligation to seek Allah's favor and mercy. Through giving to others, our faith strengthens, and we can anticipate Allah's rewards both in this life and the hereafter. Importantly, contributing to charity does not diminish our wealth; instead, spending money for the sake of Allah serves to cleanse one's spirit from the allure of material possessions.

Wealth is regarded as a divine blessing from Allah. However, when money is directed towards serving Allah, it diminishes the allure of material possessions. Spending in the path of Allah signifies that one's love for Him is the foremost priority in life, demonstrating a willingness to make any necessary compromises and sacrifices to seek His pleasure. Those who utilize their wealth to aid the impoverished and fulfill their basic needs will receive Allah's mercy.

Ensuring that one's finances are directed towards genuinely disadvantaged individuals is as crucial as giving charity itself. Hence, it is imperative to conduct thorough research before donating to ensure that your contribution reaches those in genuine need. You hold the power to decide how your donations are utilized. Therefore, when giving charity, opt for an organization that operates transparently, assists the deprived and impoverished, and adequately addresses their needs.

It's essential to remember that the poor and needy are entitled to a portion of our wealth, and it is our duty as Muslims to assist them. Whether it's a small or large contribution, what matters in the eyes of Allah is the sincerity behind the donation, not the amount.

It is widely known that money comes without instructions, therefore prioritizing our spending is worth some daily reflection. In the current recession and inflation due to wars and pandemics, living within our means has become more crucial than ever. Although, it doesn't have to mean giving up things that make life enjoyable and things you're passionate about.

Many have interpreted this as a call to reassess priorities, focusing on necessities rather than luxuries to address financial challenges. Presently, nationwide bankruptcies, asset repossessions, and job losses have reached unprecedented levels.

That's why Islam advocates for living within one's means and discourages exceeding them, as it can lead to excessive borrowing. Ideally, financial systems should prioritize values such as honesty, credibility, and transparency overindulgence and greed.

In today's context, it's crucial to be mindful of our lifestyle, utilize resources wisely, and show empathy towards those less fortunate. This is essential as we endeavor to rebuild our society and find purpose in our lives. As Muslims, we acknowledge that wealth, along with everything else in the universe, originates from and belongs to Allah.

Thus, how do we deal with our wealth accordingly?

Back in the days before Islam, the pagans would kill their children in fear of poverty. After Islam was introduced, the companions who used to practice this tradition began to abstain from it. As mentioned in our beloved Quran: "...and be good to parents, and do not kill your children because of poverty – We will give provision to you, and to them" [Quran 6:151].

God is the provider of all. A true believer does not fear poverty because they trust that God will provide for them. Some believers say that fearing poverty is the same as not trusting in God.

Muslims must earn their wealth in a lawful, or halal, way and they are blessed by Allah. Wealth shall not be earned by selling or buying things that God forbids us, such as alcohol or pork, or by engaging in illegal activities such as gambling, non-shariah compliant trading, and more. God advises them against this:

"O you who have believed, do not consume one another's wealth unjustly but only [in lawful] business by mutual consent." [Quran 4:29]

God forbids but if you happen to have money invested in impermissible investments like non-shariah compliant trading's, or bonds or stocks in companies that sell haram products, then the best course of action is to dispose of those investments and give the earnings away as sadaqah, which brings us to the next point.

The faith of Muslims is built on the five pillars of Islam and one of those pillars is giving wealth to charity, or zakat. In fact, in the Quran charity is often mentioned as going along with prayer.

"[True] righteousness is [in] one who believes in God, the Last Day, the Angels, the Book, the Prophets and gives of their wealth, in spite of love for it, to relatives, orphans, the needy, the traveler, those who ask [for help], and for freeing slaves; [and who] establishes Prayer and practices regular charity." [Quran 2:177]

The Prophet (ﷺ) set the epitome of a Muslim's generosity by generously donating his wealth to charity. Prioritizing the needs of others over his own, he exemplified simplicity and abstained from greed. Being an orphan himself, he exemplified the Quranic teachings that Muslims should allocate their wealth toward orphans and those unable to fend for themselves. Even with limited resources, one can contribute to the cause of Allah, as even the smallest donation is considered an act of charity.

When one spends his wealth in the way of God there is no decrease in wealth. Charity increases wealth because God replaces it with something better and greater. The Creator has blessed us with everything we have, so we are obligated to be intelligent and responsible in using these resources sensibly. Remember this important lesson: Happiness is not *just* about money and possessions, it's more about being responsible and accountable while living a righteous life.

There are no road maps or GPS. We just head in the direction that seems best. Purely, finding the answer by trial and error.

Looking back, Austin and his wife didn't put their marriage as a top priority. They let their kids, work, and business come first. Being a good parent was very important to them but one can't be a good parent if there was not a good marriage.

There will always be differences between Austin and his wife. But, instead of discussing them and working on them, they let them build walls. Austin expected Rihanna to prop him up with all his busyness and she expected him to prop her up with all her busyness. That wasn't possible.

They did marriage counseling but Austin was not a talky-feely guy, however, it was the best thing they could have done. If for no other reason, it made them carve out a chunk of time just for them and their marriage. It also allowed them to communicate and get advice at the same time. They have been married for 26 years now and Austin loves his wife more than ever.

The marriage counselor, an attractive girl who was just twenty-five years old, talked to Austin first as she thought talking to both Austin and Rihanna would cause issues. She introduced herself as "Rehman."

She sat in a chair opposite him and said, "Austin, we are going to do any documentation or signing up, no formal introductions and not definitely ask any questions, but tell you a story of Cuncatta."

Cuncatta was a forty-seven years old male, with a wife and three children all under six years of age. The marriage problems started when the youngest was born and involved the solemn oath taken at the time of the Islamic bond between husband and wife. A culture-based marriage with plenty of gold and food that was pleasing to the eye of the guests. The wedding took place in Birmingham, West Midlands in "The East Side" reflecting the origins of the bride from Delhi, India.

When Cuncatta was choosing a venue, he was drawn to the opening description depicting the issue at hand, to make the bride feel welcome in Birmingham.

"The Eastside Rooms is a contemporary wedding venue helping bring colour to your wedding day. They have blank canvas spaces available for up to 650 guests, making them perfect for multi-cultural weddings, including Asian and Caribbean. They also have intimate and twilight packages for more traditional celebrations. A 195-bedroom hotel is also just next door…"

It was selected as guests from New Delhi attended the wedding and the hotel was located next door.

Cuncatta was a taxi driver. He did not just drive an Uber Taxi, but he had his own black cab, an Austin FX4 with registration "CUNC 1," therefore designated and regarded as prime minister in India as the taxi drivers earned more in the UK than a prime minister in New Delhi.

Guests arrived at Birmingham International Airport by the dozen. Two flights were chartered by the bride's father as he was a contractor in New Delhi for projects undertaken by the Prime Minister's Office. However, the bride's father earned much more than Cuncatta. That's where the problem lay. In the Asian culture, it isn't recommended that the bride's family has more than a husband as it would be difficult to control the wife as the bride would be accustomed to a level of being a spendthrift.

Sarina Begum was eighteen years old and used to spending on anything and everything.

Spending money was reckless and uncontrolled. During courtship, Cuncatta explained to Sarina the story The Parable of the Prodigal Son (also known as the parable of the Two Brothers, Lost Son, Loving Father, or of the Forgiving Father) is one of the parables of Jesus in the Bible, appearing in Luke 15:11–32. Jesus shares the parable with his disciples, the Pharisees, and others.

The narrative unfolds with a father having two sons. The younger one implores his father for his share of the inheritance, which the father grants. However, this son proves to be profligate, squandering his wealth in reckless extravagance, ultimately leading to his impoverishment. Consequently, he decides to return home empty-handed, intending to beseech his father to accept him back, even as a servant. Contrary to the son's expectations, his father not only welcomes him with open arms but also throws a lavish celebration in his honor. Meanwhile, the elder son, feeling envious, refuses to partake in the festivities. In response, the father addresses him, saying, "You are ever with me, and all that I have is yours, but your younger brother was lost and now he is found."

The Parable of the Prodigal Son marks the culmination of a series on redemption, preceded by the Parable of the Lost Sheep and the Parable of the Lost Coin. Within the Revised Common Lectionary and Roman Rite Catholic Lectionary, this parable is typically read on the fourth Sunday of Lent (in Year C). In the Roman Rite Catholic Lectionary, it also forms part of the extended Gospel reading on the 24th Sunday of Ordinary Time in Year C, alongside the two preceding parables of the series. Additionally, in the Eastern Orthodox Church, it is featured on the Sunday dedicated to the Prodigal Son.

Sarina Begum was similar to the prodigal son, she wanted her inheritance whilst her father was alive. Her father obliged and she would spend shopping on-line or off-line. When Cuncatta found out it was too late to turn back the guests and send Sarina Begum back.

That marriage resulted in three children and it was a difficult seven year for both of them. Sarina wanted to return to India and Cuncatta wanted to stay working at the mini cab till the early hours of the morning and then return home to an empty house.

He would talk to his customers about his problems and listen to their problems. One customer recommended he return to India to get married through a marriage bureau, but to that he would need to divorce Sarina Begum. He quickly applied for a divorce citing his wife as a spendthrift.

According to the current divorce law, one party must file for divorce against the other, citing grounds such as adultery or unreasonable behaviour. If neither of these grounds applies, a two-year separation period with mutual consent or a five-year separation period without mutual consent is necessary.

Additionally, under the current divorce law, the Respondent has the option to contest the divorce proceedings, leading to many individuals feeling trapped in a marriage or spending substantial amounts of money in legal battles to dissolve the marriage.

The Divorce, Dissolution and Separation Act 2020 aims to reform the divorce process by minimizing potential conflict and hostility. This is achieved by eliminating the ability to make allegations about the respondent's conduct and behaviour and reducing the duration of time parties are required to remain in the marriage before seeking divorce.

No-fault divorce will be introduced into law on 6th April 2022. The key focus of the law change is to remove the fault or blame in divorce.

Cuncatta threatened Sarina Begum with the new divorce law when she didn't control her spending sprees. He was threatened in return with bailiffs and court orders and was hiding letters as soon they fell on the door mat, throwing them straight unopened into the wheelie bin. He rang the Citizens Advise Centre for advise.

The advisor spoke from the other end with a northern accent, "Bailiffs have legal powers that debt collectors do not. So if someone visits you at home about the money you owe, the first and most important thing you need to do is establish whether this is a debt collector or a bailiff. Debt collectors are not allowed to tell you that they are bailiffs, but they might be deliberately vague. That's why you should always ask to see some ID."

Cuncatta wanted to interrupt the advisor's tirade with his own questions bit the advisor went on, "If their ID says that they are a debt collector, doorstep collector or field agent, this is not a bailiff. If they are a bailiff, their ID might say 'enforcement agent' or 'enforcement officer'. You should also ask what debt they're collecting. Bailiffs may visit to collect council tax debts, child support debts, debts relating to the court (including criminal court fines and County Court Judgements, and unpaid tax or National Insurance. You won't be visited by a bailiff for credit debts like loans, catalogues or credit cards unless these debts have resulted in a CCJ."

In the seven-year marriage, Cuncatta had acquired some four County Court Judgements, thereby heading towards bankruptcy. In order to stop further slide into a river of debt, he decided to part company with Sarina.

Notwithstanding the children's need for a father figure, he took the passenger's advise and contacted the number in New Delhi and made arrangements to travel to India with the only credit card he hadn't maxed out.

In New Delhi, he was picked up directly from the airport and taken to a small town, weaving through the traffic and nearly crashing with a truck.

"Can't they drive normally here?" Cuncatta yelled out loud as the driver took the truck past his car.

"This is normal, abnormal is when they drive properly," the bearded driver shouted back at him with a grin.

X – 3

Theranos Inc. (/ˈθɛr.ən.oʊs/), founded in 2003 by 19-year-old Elizabeth Holmes, was an American privately held corporation hailed as a revolutionary health technology company. It garnered over US$700 million from venture capitalists and private investors, reaching a peak valuation of $10 billion in 2013 and 2014. The company asserted it had pioneered blood tests requiring minuscule samples and offering rapid, accurate results through compact automated devices it had developed. However, these assertions were later found to be untrue.

Misrepresentation was universally condemned across religions due to its moral reprehensibility, as it misled individuals into a false sense of security.

Legally, the crucial aspect revolved around establishing intent, raising the question whether Theranos was promoted primarily for financial gains or to provide genuine medical assistance to individuals with serious illnesses.

During her time at Stanford University, Elizabeth Holmes conceived the notion of creating a wearable patch capable of regulating drug dosage and alerting physicians to fluctuations in patients' blood parameters. She initiated the development of lab-on-a-chip technology for blood testing, envisioning a company that would revolutionize the affordability, convenience, and accessibility of such tests for consumers.

In 2003, Holmes left Stanford and utilized the educational fund provided by her parents to establish the company, later named Theranos, a blend of "therapy" and "diagnosis". Initially named "Real-Time Cures," Holmes opted for the change as she felt the term "cure" generated excessive skepticism.

In 2012, Safeway allocated $350 million towards outfitting 800 of its locations with clinics intended to offer in-store blood tests. Following numerous missed deadlines and dubious outcomes from a trial clinic at Safeway's corporate headquarters, the agreement was terminated in 2015. Concurrently, in 2013, Theranos forged a partnership with Walgreens to provide in-store blood tests at over 40 locations. Despite reports of Theranos blood tests being utilized on participants in drug trials conducted by GlaxoSmithKline and Pfizer, both companies clarified in October 2015 that they had no ongoing projects with Theranos. Subsequently, in June 2016, Walgreens terminated its association with Theranos, leading to a legal dispute wherein Walgreens filed a breach of contract lawsuit against Theranos in federal court in Delaware in November 2016. By June 2017, Theranos informed investors that the lawsuit, initially seeking $140 million in damages, was settled for under $30 million.

In March 2015, the Cleveland Clinic unveiled a partnership with Theranos aimed at evaluating its technology and reducing the expenses associated with laboratory tests. Additionally, in July 2015, Theranos secured contracts to serve as the lab services provider for Pennsylvania insurers AmeriHealth Caritas and Capital Blue Cross.

In July 2015 the Food and Drug Administrationapproved the use of the company's fingerstick blood testing device for the herpes simplex virus (HSV-1) outside a clinical laboratory setting. Theranos was named the 2015 Bioscience Company of the Year by the Arizona BioIndustry Association (AzBio).

"It was just another Silicon Valley startup gone wrong." Austin said to his wife on the phone.

"Another con in the cruel world we live in where politicians and military take advantage of the general public," Rihanna replied.

"There must be someone who does," Austin commented.

Rihanna sighed over the line as she said, "It's like the homeless people, ironically she was called 'Holmes,' but with all the money in the world she didn't care about homes. The politicians didn't care after hearing 'Holmes' in the news, the papers, Forbes magazine. It was a constant reminder to people in power to hear the God's message. All the politicians and military board members thought about was how to line their pockets quickly and easily. They forgot about the patients and the patients, which in Islam is a command of Allah."

Austin hummed, "It was just another day in paradise for the board members whilst homeless people suffered because their parents couldn't reach them."

Holmes started to work with the "Clintons" to host charity events to support her falsehood. The satan's work wasn't complete to show the falsehood, hated by Allah is alive under the satan. The "Health Matters Campaign" was a cover up for falsehood and manipulated by Holmes and her husband, Sunny Balwani. As a Hindu he believed in falsehood of God and in real life that was replicated by destroying the lives many thousands as their invention gave false sense of security. The belief of the Ten Commandments wasn't followed and replication in life is a dangerous step. To idolise God, is a sin as it gives rise to falsehood. Everyone has a bit of God in them from the first breath they take, oxygen provided by the creator to give them life, to help people less weak than themselves, not to abuse life and destroy the weak amongst society.

"So, what did you get up to today?" Austin asked.

Rihanna chuckled, "The dishwasher is still talking in French, the fridge in Japanese and the washing machine in Arabic."

"You should either learn the language or call the supplier to come and fix it."

"They're charging a fortune, I think I better learn the languages," Rihanna replied.

"I thought you were learning Arabic?"

"I am but it's only one day a week for two hours for ten weeks at the University."

"That's not bad," Austin noted.

"It's not good either. I want to re-write the hadeeths into something people understand," Rihanna admitted.

"But, there's millions of them. Why don't you learn one line?"

"What's that?"

"Be a good person and help others," Austin said.

"Why?"

Austin explained, "Because at judgment day the Almighty will ask two questions. Firstly, what was your intention? And secondly, how did it help the community? It is easy if you try."

"I think the teacher bloke has taken a liking to me. He fancies my rolling of the tongue."

"Hang on, that was my idea!" Austin retorted.

"What idea?" Rihanna asked with a smirk.

"How to roll your tongue," Austin muttered.

Rihanna scoffed over the line, "It was mine, I taught you."

"It was also my idea to get a website "FB man (&mens) UK Ltd."

"What's FB?"

"Facebook."

"Okay, run it past me again."

"To use the platform to target men who want to go to the UK and get married to divorcees and widows. It's a great reward from Allah to get them married."

"But, I'm not divorced or widowed?" Rihanna asked.

"You do call yourself a "married widow on FB don't you? I check your posts."

"That's just a way of expressing my feelings to the outside world."

"Yeah, but there's a lot of men out there that will take advantage of that,"

"And women."

"What do mean women?"

"There's a lot of women in the same boat."

"Surely, you mean bed?"

"No, I don't swing both ways."

"I've seen you look at women."

"I've seen you look at women too." Rihanna commented pointing at him.

"It's surely better than looking at men."

Allah has ordained the eye as the reflection of the heart. When a person restrains their gaze, their heart maintains control over their desires and intentions. Conversely, if one allows their gaze to roam freely, their heart will grant unchecked sway to their desires. In the authenticated narrations, it is recounted that during the Day of Sacrifice, al-Fadl ibn 'Abbaas (may Allah be pleased with him) journeyed from Muzdalifah to Mina, where he encountered some women, prompting him to gaze upon them.

Upon witnessing this, the Messenger of Allah (peace and blessings of Allah be upon him) turned his face away. Ibn al-Qayyim remarked in Rawdat al-Muhibbeen that this incident highlights the prohibition of looking at non-mahram women, underscoring its practical condemnation. Had looking been permissible, the Prophet (peace and blessings of Allah be upon him) would have endorsed it.

In al-Saheeh it is narrated that [the Prophet] (peace and blessings of Allah be upon him) said: "Allah has decreed for the son of Adam his share of zina which will inevitably come to him. The eye commits zina and its zina is looking. The tongue commits zina and its zina is speaking. The foot commits zina and its zina is walking. The hand commits zina and its zina is touching. The heart longs and wishes, and the private part confirms that or denies it."

"He started with the zina of the eye because it is the basis of the zina of the hand, foot, heart and private part. And the zina of the mouth by kissing is implied by the reference to the zina of the mouth by speaking. And he described the private part as confirming that if the action is fulfilled, or denying it if it is not. He said: This hadeeth is one of the clearest signs that the eye can sin by looking, and that this is its zina. This is a refutation of those who permit letting the gaze wander freely." Rihanna quoted.

Austin contemplated over her words before answering, "But, there is something that I can't stop as I work in the construction industry and all I see are unshaven guys all day long. So, it's difficult not look."

"You don't look, you stare and then start drooling, and I can see you pulling in your stomach."

"It's only the first unintentional look, it's not like I'm jumping into bed with them."

"As for looking unintentionally, one will not be punished for that if the heart did not intend it, but if he follows it with another look, then he is sinning."

"So, it's okay for woman to look at another woman and a man to look at another man?"

"Exactly, that way men aren't committing any sin," Rihanna clarified.

"Now, isn't that promoting the wrong message about homosexuality?"

"Islam doesn't promote same sex marriage, so eventually when you look at a woman then the intention should be to marry her."

"That means I will have to marry nearly a million women. I don't think that's fair." Austin frowned.

"Okay, let me put it another way."

"Gone on," Austin prompted Rihanna.

"A man rode into town and stopped at a saloon for a drink. Unfortunately, the locals always had a habit of picking on strangers, which he was. When he finished his drink, he found his bike and his wife had been stolen. He went back into the bar, handily flipped a coin into air, caught it above his head without even looking and then snapped the coin into two with his teeth. *'Which one of you sinners stole my bike and wife?!'* he yelled with surprising forcefulness. No one answered. Then he said, *'Ok, I'll have another pint, but let me tell you guys, I don't want to do what I did in Manchester the other week. Let me tell you guys I didn't like what I did in Manchester and have nightmares about it.'* When he finished his pint and walked outside, he saw both his wife and the bike back in the place he left them," Rihanna paused for dramatic effect, then continued, "The bar tender rushed after him before he could give his wife a crossbar and ride away. *'So what happened in Manchester?'* The barman asked, slightly worried. *'Not much, I lost both my wife and bike and I had to walk home and find another wife.'*[x]"

Rihanna paused after telling the story and waited for Austin's reaction.

After a beat of silence, Austin replied, "That's not funny at all."

"Okay, this one you'd love."

"Fine, nearly suicidal here." Warned Austin.

Rihanna continued further, "A man walks into a bar with a bag and orders a drink. After a while, the bartender asks him, *'What is in the bag?'* The man says, *'Nothing, don't worry about it.'* The night continues and the bartender keeps asking but the man keeps giving him the same answer. A man walks into a bar with a bag and orders a drink. After a while, the bartender asks him, *'What is in the bag?'* The man says, *'Nothing, don't worry about it.'* The night continues and the bartender keeps asking but the man keeps giving him the same answer. Towards the end of the night the bartender offers the man a free beer if the man shows him what is in the bag. The man agrees. He reaches into the bag and pulls out a tiny piano and a tiny man that sits down and starts playing the piano. The bartender says, *'Wow! That's amazing! Where did you find they guy?'* The man looks up and says, *'I have this magic lamp that grants me wishes, but the stupid thing is broken.'* The man then hands the bartender the lamp and says, *'You can try it if you want.'* The bartender happily grabs the lamp and wishes for a million pounds and the room is suddenly filled with a million sounds. *'This thing is definitely broken!'* says the bartender."

"Seriously?" Austin questioned.

"Yeah, I know a lot more."

"What more jokes than FB Man(and Mens) UK Limited?"

"What's this new argument?"

"It's not an argument, but I have checking your Facebook account and out of frustration I came up with a new idea."

"Oh, one of those again."

Austin explained that if he set up a website and targeted the men in Third World countries a glimpse of life in the United Kingdom offering women who were recently divorced or widowed and a proper job for a fixed fee of five thousand pounds. He can then make a bit of a business out of it. Rihanna complained that Austin might disappear with one of the women on offer. After two decades Austin pointed out that she was insecure.

"You mean sham marriages?" asked Rihanna.

"No, our service will be a genuine intent and interest and it's up to the men to enter a marriage as Islam rewards such good deeds."

Although labeled as a "sham" or "fake" due to its underlying motives, the union retains legal validity if it adheres to the formal legal prerequisites for marriage within the jurisdiction. However, orchestrating or participating in such a marriage with the intent to mislead public authorities constitutes a legal offense in certain countries, such as the United States.

Following a duration, couples frequently pursue divorce if there is no longer any rationale for staying married. Conversely, the scenario wherein a couple obtains a divorce while continuing to cohabit is commonly referred to as a "sham" marriage.

Frequently, sham marriages are pursued with the aim of acquiring immigration, residency, employment, or citizenship privileges for one of the partners.

There have been instances where individuals entered into sham marriages to deflect suspicions regarding their sexual orientation, including cases in Hollywood where homosexual or homoromantic actors like Rock Hudson were purportedly urged by studios to conceal their homosexuality through what became known as "lavender marriages."

Since the convergence of marriage-based citizenship laws and accessible international travel in the latter part of the 20th century, sham marriages have emerged as a prevalent method for facilitating a foreign national's residency, and potentially citizenship, in the more desirable country of their spouse. The involved couple typically acknowledges that the marriage serves solely as a means of obtaining advantageous immigration status, with no intention of living as a genuine couple. Such arrangements often transpire as business transactions involving monetary exchanges and are more frequent among foreigners already present in the country.

Since the implementation of the Home Office's hostile environment policy in 2012, there has been widespread criticism in the UK regarding heavy-handed measures impacting legitimate marriages. Authentic wedding ceremonies have been disrupted, and early morning raids have been conducted to ascertain whether couples are cohabiting. Individuals have been detained for extended periods after being falsely accused of engaging in sham marriages. In 2018, the Home Office investigated 1,618 marriages flagged as suspicious by registrars; however, they declined to disclose the number determined to be sham.

In 2013, the Home Office estimated that between 4,000 and 10,000 marriages annually were sham unions established to secure legal immigration status for the non-EU partner. Assuming an average of 500 such marriages per month, each with fees of £2000, this indicates a potential market worth nearly ten million pounds per month.

"You'll get banged up!" Rihanna shouted over the phone.

"I don't think so as our intention is right and marriage is part of the hadeeth that every Muslim should be married to go forth and multiply. That's the reason why I look at women as it's a command from God to go forth and multiply."

"That's the worse cop out I've ever heard," Rihanna put the phone down without wishing Austin to take care, which she would normally.

X – 4

Nikha: The Marriage

Enemies used to take prisoners of war from Mecca to Medina. At Mecca, there was a prostitute called 'Inaq' who had illicit relations with one of the enemies who later went to the Prophet and said to him: "May I marry Inaq, Messenger of Allah?"

The Prophet replied, "Yes you may marry her as long as she accepts you as a husband and you accept her sins."

The enemy asked, "What about my slave?"

The prophet replied, "Yes, free her from slavery and your reward will double."

Prophet Mohammed emphasizes the importance of marriage by saying: *"A person who can support a wife and children and does not marry, then he is not from us."*

Austin knew by virtue that having a wife was to increase one's faith and belief, but his ex-wife wasn't his choice, he was forced into marriage. The second marriage wasn't that good either and over time he realized that the first marriage wasn't that bad. Daphne his first wife suffered from bipolar dysfunction and required constant attention. After the children were born Daphne had an episode. Austin didn't know what to do, so they went to the family doctor who had known Daphne's father for decades. Austin was informed of the illness that Daphne had developed the illness in her late teens.

Austin had married Daphne in the early twenties.

When the doctor told him how Daphne had been diagnosed before their marriage, Austin sighed and said, "Thank God, Dr. Abida, I thought it was down to me?"

Dr. Abida passed him a reassuring smile, "Don't worry! With the correct medication, she'll be fine. I did prescribe them in 1979."

"What medicine? I never saw her take any tablets," Austin asked, confused.

"I will prescribe a month's supply of Olanzapine."

"Can I take one? I feel depressed as no one told me about this."

"Why didn't her father tell you?" Dr Abida looked at Austin sternly.

"No idea doctor, but we have three children and I want her to get better for the children."

"It's hard work, don't take it lightly, and make sure your wife takes it daily."

"Daily? I thought you said monthly for Mentali."

"It's not for Mentli it's for Daphne. Who's Mentali?"

"It's her new nickname, we have to be friends with the enemy? Don't we? Call it nicknames to make it sound better like people with cancer call it nicknames."

"Are you on some medication as well?"

"No, never had a tablet in my life."

"I think I should refer you to a specialist."

"Why me?"

"No. for Mentali, oh god you got me saying it now. And I nearly put Mentali on the prescription. Where did you get married?"

"Can't remember I think I was doped."

"Don't you mean duped?"

"No definitely doped. I wanted a simple marriage in a mosque for instance, though the Nikah ceremony traditionally takes place in a mosque, with the leader or imam of the mosque officiating the ceremony, today, it is common to have the Nikah either at a venue or at the bride's house. Moreover, although the Nikah ceremony is intended to remain modest to avoid imposing financial strain on the couple, it often evolves into a lavish affair as individuals blend Islamic and Western customs."

Dr. Abida seemed even more interested and asked, "So what happened?"

"It was a town hall with at least five hundred people."

"I was there, I remember now."

"Why didn't you stop the 'Nikah'?"

"It wasn't my place to."

"Of course, sorry for that," Austin apologized with his hand on his heart and then pointed to the ceiling, saying "He sees all, hears all, and does nothing at all to stop these things happening."

"I am sure he does, but patience is a virtue, good things come to those who wait to appreciate his miracles."

"Well, I need a miracle cure now in a physical form. I think I just sold my life and love for free." Austin said.

"There are no tablets for a miracle, but they do happen. Lead her to prayer than a dance floor."

"I rather lead her to the dance floor, that cures my issues and forget things like dancing blues away. But I have guilty feet and no rhythm."

"Why?"

"I shouldn't have cheated my ex-girlfriend. Wasted the chance I had been given."

"It's difficult I can see you're getting upset."

"So, I'm never going to dance again, the way I danced with her."

"Time can mend," Dr Abida tried to give Austin hope.

"There's no comfort in the truth, pain is all I find, without her love. Though it's easy to pretend that I am over her, even after three kids I dream about her."

Doctor Abida continued but in a soft calming way, "In many ways, the Nikah Nama is like a prenuptial agreement. It contains a series of terms that apply during marriage, death, or divorce. Don't you remember talking to anyone or your parents about which clauses they should include in your Nikah Nama? You didn't know you could do that… or should do that. But put it this way. You wouldn't sign a mortgage agreement without reading it, would you?"

Austin nodded before adding, "It was a difficult time for me as I wasn't sure and confused. There were tears and more tears as the whole family was involved. In the end, I gave in."

Austin left the surgery slightly bewildered and now with three children to take care of, he wanted to clarify his responsibilities as a father.

The key to a family's prosperity lies in the manner in which one cares for their wife. This responsibility, akin to the duty of a woman toward her husband, which is esteemed to be as significant as Jihad, is also considered the noblest and most valuable action for a man. However, a married man must strive to treat his wife in a manner that transforms her into an angelic figure.

To achieve this, a man should familiarize himself with his wife's behavior and desires. He should structure his life around her wishes and virtuous requests. Through his own conduct and demeanor, he can positively influence her, sparking her interest in both himself and their household.

Some of these roles are done with materials while others are immaterial. Among the material roles are: "Giving the wife her dower. This is one of the duties of the husband that must be fulfilled before the marriage can be considered legal. The dower is given in any materials the woman prefers. It may be money, pieces of jewelry, or other materials. Its mode of payment depends on the agreement between both parties. It may be paid in installments. It may also be deferred. The ideal woman may also return part of the dower to his husband. At the same time, it may be paid immediately before the contract is sealed. Whichever way it takes it is a right of the woman and the duty of the man that must not be jettisoned."

The Good Book says: "And give the women their gift graciously. But if they give up willingly to you anything of it, then take it in satisfaction and ease."

The responsibility to provide for the upkeep of his wife, as outlined in the previously mentioned verse of the Qur'an, falls upon the man. This encompasses providing for her nourishment, clothing, shelter, services, healthcare, and all the expenses necessary to ensure the welfare of the household.

Forty years ago, fathers shouldered significant responsibility for their children, especially since religion was openly taught in schools. However, with subsequent changes to the educational system, this religious instruction diminished, leading to a loss of guidance and discipline in the lives of children. Religion gradually became a relic of the past, paving the way for feelings of depression among individuals and communities. Money and the pursuit of wealth began to overshadow religious values. Parents retained the right to decline their children's attendance in these classes.

When Austin converted to Islam, he was keen to perform a Nikah, but without a ceremony, as he always taught that it was first of all important for him to perform the Nikah as he wanted to start a life. The only problem was her father served under Hitler as his right-hand man. Not much was talked about after that apart from her father owning a lot of land in Germany but when Rihanna was four, he had disappeared.

It was a sour subject when it was accidentally brought up during a heated argument. It was the same as any topic relating to Chelsea was bought up when they were below fourth position in the premiership. At times a lot of silence was met with "Eat your vegetables now!" resembling the tension.

The hadeeth was broken many times and Austin would constantly remind Rihanna. She would then argue that Hadeeth may be right. And the mother is always right.

"Seriously?" Austin asked.

"Exactly. The reality is that certain parents exhibit excessive control and high demands, often referred to as "tiger parenting." In some cases, they may even display cruelty and abuse toward their children. The notion that children must obey their parents stems from the belief that parents, with their wisdom and life experience, have their children's best interests at heart. However, not all parents fulfill this ideal. Is it morally wrong to refuse unreasonable demands from such parents? What does disobedience entail in such contexts?" Austin asked Rihanna.

With that in mind, Austin dozed off, hoping that Chelsea had a slight chance of getting into Europe rather than Rihanna bringing a good parent.

In the morning, Austin reminded Rihanna of the solemn oath they both took some two decades ago.

"We took an oath that I took you to be my wife to have and to hold from this day forward, for better, for worse, for richer, for poorer, in sickness and in health, to love and to cherish, till death, us do part, according to God's holy law. In the presence of God, I make this vow."

"So?" Rihanna asked, arching a brow at him.

"It means to till death not because a child is not eating his vegetables."

In Islamic Law, 'Nikah' is defined as a contractual union between two individuals of opposite genders who were previously strangers, formalizing their relationship and mutual cohabitation. This contract entails specific responsibilities and grants certain rights to both partners, delineating the roles of father and mother. However, nowhere does it stipulate that a child must consume vegetables.

Rihanna turned her back and pretended to sleep.

"The Torah addresses the topic of marriage in various passages. For instance, the book of Genesis narrates the initial union between Adam and Eve. Subsequently, in the book of Exodus, instructions are given to the Israelites to marry within their own tribe. The book of Leviticus contains numerous laws pertaining to marriage, including regulations on permissible unions and proper marital conduct. Lastly, in the book of Deuteronomy, there is a well-known passage discussing the permissibility of a man having multiple wives. Thus, marriage is a recurring theme in the Torah, indicating its significant importance to the Israelites," by the time Austin finished the last sentence, Rihanna was snoring.

Austin got out the bed and made his way to the kitchen to make a cup of coffee. He found more comfort in the cup of coffee than Rihanna and reminded him of when he first met her, warm and gentle reminding like the Nescafé Gold Blend, as time passed she had turned into Nescafé De-Caffeinated and then in the last few months into an Irish Coffee.

Austin didn't realise how a person could change so much over two decades.

When she decided to enter politics she had turned from a gentle, sweet girl into a bitter and twisted woman. It worried Austin how their two sons would see their mother in her new role as standing up for the seat at Leicester Forest East in her pinstripe suit smelling like an English rose and defending her German father who was Hitler's right-hand man.

Adolf Hitler, born in Austria and later becoming a German politician, held dictatorial power in Germany from 1933 until his suicide in 1945. He ascended to leadership as the head of the Nazi Party, assuming the position of chancellor in 1933 before later adopting the title of Führer und Reichskanzler in 1934.

Rihanna, like any girl, adored her father and mother, and when he passed away when she was just four was constantly on her mind.

Austin felt her father's death when she explained and when he had the chance to speak to his mother-in-law. Rihanna always said to her mother that Austin reminded her of her father, the way Austin was kind to people and those who he loved and lived for. Totally different from Adolf's life which her father hated, but supported.

Upon attaining power, Hitler dismantled the nation's democratic institutions and converted Germany into a militarized state with ambitions of conquering Europe in favor of the purported Aryan race. During the invasion of Poland, Nazi military units targeted and executed approximately 11 million individuals deemed inferior or undesirable, categorized as "life unworthy of life," including Jews, Slavs, homosexuals, and Jehovah's Witnesses.

Hitler garnered support from German officer-class households and numerous ordinary citizens who voted for the National Socialist German Workers' Party, celebrating him as a national savior during massive stadium rallies.

Hitler ascended to power through the Nazi Party, an entity he established after returning as a wounded veteran from the devastating trench warfare of World War I. Alongside other patriotic Germans, he harbored deep resentment and humiliation over the harsh conditions imposed by the Treaty of Versailles.

Forced upon the new German government, the Weimar Republic, by the Allies, the treaty mandated Germany to pay $33 billion in war reparations. Additionally, Germany was compelled to relinquish its prized overseas colonies and cede valuable territories to France and Poland. The German military underwent significant downsizing, and the nation was prohibited from possessing submarines or an air force. As one British official bluntly stated, "We shall squeeze the German lemon until the pips squeak!"

The burden of paying the overwhelming reparations led to economic instability, resulting in catastrophic hyperinflation. By September 1923, four billion German marks were equivalent to just one American dollar. Consumers found themselves needing a wheelbarrow to transport enough paper money to purchase a single loaf of bread.

Hitler, known for his captivating oratory skills, delivered speeches at political gatherings in Munich, advocating for a new German framework to supplant what he perceived as an inept and ineffective democratic government. This envisioned New Order entailed an authoritarian political model characterized by a hierarchical leadership system in which authority emanated downward from a supreme national leader.

Austin comforted himself with the thought that everyone has a bit of Hitler in them and it was the media who protested against him that brought the scenes into viewers' minds and Austin's phrase, "See no evil, hear no evil, and do no evil," obviously had failed for Rihanna.

He made another cup of coffee as the hair on the back of his neck stood up as he contemplated the thought of Rihanna becoming an MP with her beautiful angelic face. Austin was glad there was an angel of mercy in God's team on Earth in Rihanna.

She attracted both men and women and explained in her great command of English how they should be family people and care for their children and there was still an ounce of Nescafé Gold Blend left in her, but still had a pound of Hitler in her.

He decided to make her cup of coffee as a peace offering under the written law of the hadeeth for marriage.

X – 5

Yakub

Jakob was a Polish Engineer and Austin's good friend, short of being his best friend. They met when they were building Peterborough General Hospital, named after the nurse Edith Carvell.

Edith Carvell was celebrated for her impartial care of wounded soldiers from all factions during World War I, as well as her role in aiding around 200 Allied soldiers in escaping from German-occupied Belgium. However, she was arrested, subjected to a court-martial under German military jurisdiction, and ultimately sentenced to death by firing squad. Despite widespread international appeals for clemency, the German authorities declined to alter her sentence, leading to her execution. This act provoked global outrage and garnered extensive media attention.

The evening preceding her execution, she expressed, "Patriotism is not enough. I must have no hatred or bitterness towards anyone." These sentiments were engraved on the Edith Cavell Memorial close to Trafalgar Square. Her steadfast Anglican convictions motivated her to aid all individuals in need, irrespective of their allegiance, be they German or Allied soldiers. She was noted for declaring, "I can't stop while there are lives to be saved."

Cavell was born on December 4, 1865, in Swardeston, a village situated near Norwich, where her father served as the vicar for a remarkable 45 years. She was the eldest among the four offspring of the Reverend Frederick Cavell (1824–1910) and his wife, Louisa Sophia Warming (1835–1918). Edith's siblings included Florence Mary (1867-1950), Mary Lilian (1870-1967), and John Frederick Scott (1872–1923).

Cavell was educated at Norwich High School for Girls, then at boarding schools in Clevedon, Somerset, and Peterborough(Laurel Court).

Following a stint as a governess, which included working for a family in Brussels from 1890 to 1895, Cavell returned home to tend to her father during a severe illness. This experience prompted her to pursue a career in nursing after her father recuperated. Joining the Fountain Fever Hospital in Tooting in December 1895, Cavell began her nursing journey. At the age of 30, she applied to enter the nursing probation program at the London Hospital and commenced her training as a regular probationer under Matron Eva Luckes in September 1896. During her probationary period, Cavell was assigned to assist other London Hospital nurses during the Maidstone typhoid epidemic, from October 15, 1897, until early January 1898.

Despite still being in her probationary phase, Cavell and her colleagues were honored with the Maidstone Typhoid Medal for their efforts. Upon completing her training, Cavell served as a private nurse employed by the Private Nursing Institution of the London Hospital from October 1898 to December 1899, offering care to patients in their homes. Her nursing duties encompassed attending to individuals with various ailments such as cancer, gout, pneumonia, pleurisy, eye conditions, and appendicitis.

In 1901, Luckes recommended Cavell for the position of night superintendent of St Pancras Infirmary.

In November 1914, following the German occupation of Brussels, Cavell initiated the clandestine operation of harboring British soldiers and facilitating their escape from occupied Belgium to the neutral Netherlands.

Under the protection of Prince Réginald de Croÿ at his château of Bellignies near Mons, wounded British and French soldiers, along with Belgian and French civilians of military age, were concealed from German forces and supplied with counterfeit documents. Subsequently, they were guided by various individuals to the residences of Cavell, Louis Séverin, and others in Brussels.

Here, they received financial assistance to reach the Dutch border and were provided with guides coordinated by Philippe Baucq. Cavell's involvement in these activities contravened German military regulations. As a result, German authorities grew increasingly suspicious of her actions, exacerbated by her outspokenness.

On August 3, 1915, Cavell was apprehended and accused of harboring Allied soldiers. Her arrest stemmed from betrayal by Georges Gaston Quien, who was subsequently convicted by a French court for collaboration. Cavell was incarcerated in Saint-Gilles prison for a duration of ten weeks, with the final two weeks spent in solitary confinement.

During this time, she provided three statements to the German authorities (on August 8, 18, and 22), wherein she acknowledged her role in facilitating the passage of approximately 60 British and 15 French soldiers, along with around 100 French and Belgian civilians of military age, to the border. Additionally, she admitted to providing shelter to most of them in her residence.

During her court-martial, Cavell faced charges of assisting British and French soldiers, as well as young Belgian men, in crossing the Dutch border with the eventual aim of reaching Britain. She acknowledged her culpability by signing a statement the day prior to the trial.

Cavell asserted that the soldiers she aided expressed their gratitude in written form upon safely arriving in Britain. This acknowledgment validated Cavell's involvement in guiding the soldiers across the Dutch border, while also establishing that she facilitated their escape to a nation engaged in conflict with Germany.

According to German military law, the punishment for such offenses was death. As per Paragraph 58 of the German Military Code, it was stipulated that "in time of war, anyone who with the intention of aiding a hostile power, or of causing harm to German or allied troops" commits any of the crimes defined in Paragraph 90 of the German Penal Code "shall be punished with death for war treason".

In Cavell's case, she was indicted under Paragraph 90 (1) no. 3 Reichsstrafgesetzbuch for "conveying troops to the enemy", a transgression typically met with a sentence of life imprisonment in times of peace.

It was possible to charge Cavell with perfidy, or war treason (German: Kriegsverrat), as paragraph 160 of the German Military Code extended the application of paragraph 58 to foreigners "present in the zone of war".

Yakub's wife, Latifah, was a Moroccan nurse who found a job in Dubai and eventually married a local doctor. They had two children but after a few years, the doctor had become abusive and controlling. Latifah had no choice other than to tolerate such behaviour, constantly reminding him that the prophets were all men and kind to their wives.

The Doctor mostly replied along the lines of, "Of course, they were as paying alimony for numerous wives would've bankrupted them. So the hadeeths were written as everyday lives of the prophet. In Dubai, the men buy a property with at least four floors and the oldest wife resides at the highest level as a sign of respect. The youngest one resides on the ground floor."

Latifah was shocked to hear his words. "Is that because the oldest wife is closer to God?" she asked.

"No, because the oldest wife will probably have arthritis and it's best to keep her up there so as not to get jealous of the youngest wife," the doctor replied.

Latifah shook her head, "That's terrible."

The doctor thought for a few moments then said, "Hang on, the youngest wife will cook food and take it up to the oldest wife's a peace offering and they will be good friends."

"Silly as it sounds, but that does make sense in a horrible kind of way."

When the doctor said he was buying a house with seven floors, Latifah decided to find a new husband.

Yakub was wondering whether he should start visiting nightclubs with Austin and that was when he met Latifah. Yakub was going through a separation and was trying hard to get his estranged wife to start a new life in Dubai.

In 2007, the new metro was being constructed so traffic was always slow-moving as third-country nationals lived in Sharjah or Ajman as the rents were considerably low. So Yakub rented an apartment near Taweelah, an industrial area between Abu Dhabi and Dubai. The area Yakub rented was isolated and the roads were still not completed.

Yakub and Austin worked long hours and both of their respective marriages were under strain. They both were technical engineers in the quest for turning seawater into drinking water through reverse osmosis.

It involved the construction of steelwork which housed filters that would remove contaminates found in sea water and then went to an already constructed desalination plant to remove the brine from the water. The working conditions put both Yakub and Austin off water and they started having a drink after long and painful hours on site.

Yakub would return late to his isolated wife. There were obvious arguments and threats to return to the United Kingdom, but Yakub said he was fed up with the miserable life she had made. His twelve-year-old son cried to sleep most nights.

Austin was in the same boat and Rihanna was approached by many Arabic men who followed her every time she went to the malls. Both Yakub and Austin decided to float a business named "FB (man) & (men's) UK Ltd based on their life experiences with women and what they want.

The initial registration was 99p with a 30-minute initial interview on Skype. They were using technology to help men and women become one entity and eventually live in the United Kingdom.

The first month wasn't great as it was Ramadhan and it was considered sinful to talk about marriage, but a month of reflection and being close to God. After Ramadhan the website was very active and Austin in his Queen's English impressed the men and conquered the women by taking them to the next level of actually meeting in Dubai.

However, he would charge a nominal fee of £250 from each couple but charged £28 per hour if he had to be a chaperone. As a separated man, he found joy in getting people together. The next level was marriage, accommodation, and income. Austin would charge £42 per hour negotiating with wedding venues, estate agents, and recruiters. However, Austin would cap the costs at £7,500 per couple.

He would convince the couple if they stayed married for 20 years. That would equate to £1.07 per day, which was slightly more than the 99p registration fee, however, with that the couple could get a council house, universal credit, and a lovely family in a beautiful country.

Yakub dropped out of the business citing that Latifah was pregnant and he didn't know if he was the father or the doctor. Either way, he had fallen in love with Latifah. Yakub looked more depressed than usual while Austin was glowing.

With business booming, he decided to expand the business by arranging a yearly review with himself to see how they were getting on without any fury fees. He called it, "A Free MOT for life. I mean people have MOTs for cars, warranties for electrical items, so why not for marriage?"

That was a unique selling point.

When Yakub returned to England from Dubai and married Latifah he struggled to get a spouse visa as his estranged wife wouldn't divorce him due to the financial settlement so Austin offered her an employment visa as a French translator.

Again, Yakub suffered as Latifah continued to spend money as if she was living in Dubai and credit card debt got out of hand, Yakub turned to Austin and advised, "Austerity At Home."

"Don't you mean Austin at home?"

"Yes, it comes what I did."

"Meaning?" asked Yakub looking confused.

"Use the golden rule of 50-30-20"

"Okay, are you going to elaborate?"

"Needs, Wants and Savings."

"That's as useful as a broken clock."

"Needs are Utility bills, housing, and groceries while wants are vacations, Take-Aways, Alcohol, and Fags while Savings is the money you put into a pension."

"What savings?" Latifah interrupted and showed a Morrisons receipt.

Now Austin looked confused, but asked, "253 pounds for a grocery bill and 2p savings?"

"Yes, 2p savings."

"No, why 253 pounds?"

"We have 3 children all under six, they need feeding, clothing, and cleaning," Latifah replied rather aggressively.

Austin huffed, "Remember I was poor once, I mean working man is always poor unless the woman is working. If not then 50-30-20 becomes the golden rule. Do you have a flip chart?"

"Yes in the children's bedroom," Yakub rushed off to bring it.

By the time, Yakub returned Austin had drilled into Latifah that it was the wife's job to cut costs and a husband's job to provide income like "Lucy the Chimp.'"

"Lucy the chimp," Latifah muttered unconvincingly.

Austin nodded, "Yes, the human-chimp who was crazy but soon saw sense. Anyway, let me draw a few pictures."

"What pictures?"

"Lucy," Austin replied simply.

Austin drew a chimpanzee and a gorilla. "Let's call the gorilla, 'Gorah,'" he said after he finished the drawing.

"What housing costs did Gorah and Lucy have?"

"None."

"What grocery bills did they have?"

"None."

"What utility bills did they have."

"None."

"So 50% rule met."

"Okay 30% was?" asked Austin.

"Wants!" All the kids shouted together.

"Vacations? None, Fags? None, Alcohol? None and lastly take-aways or restaurants?None."

"Savings – None as there was no income, so no debt a cumulated."

"Do you want us to live like animals?" Latifah asked.

Austin shook his head, "No, but spend a little, save a lot for your children, not for yourself."

Austin drew a large pound sign, a television, a sofa, a Christmas tree, and presents under the tree. Then he said, "Now Lucy and Gorah have become humans and humans have invented money. Gorah goes out to work and Lucy stays at home watching TV all day long."

"How do TV channels make money?"

"License fee!," Children shouted again.

"Wrong this time!" Austin exclaimed.

"Advertising branded items, not Primark or corner shops or small businesses. They don't want the customers to pay for the extra margin. Because the adverts are financed through loans from the banks."

"Now it's getting complicated," Yakub commented.

"No, it's simple in order to get a massive turnover and little profit they have to target working families but the cost of weekly shop goes up as they create demand. Brands push down the price of buying goods by making sure farmers go out of business. Anyway, we are moving away from the objective of the exercise and boring the hell out of the children. Let's take an income of a thousand pounds."

Austin drew the number.

"So 50% is £500, 30% is £300 and 20% is £200"

"No one gets £1000"

"They do single parents on benefits."

"So can you rent a flat or house, pay utility bills or groceries for £500? Probably not."

Austin paused.

"Can they take away or eat in the restaurant for £300? Probably can and drink alcohol and fags? Just about, I would say."

"Can they save £200? Probably not. What we end up is with misguided by the TV in order for companies to make money to pay the interest on the loans and loans are?"

"Haraam," Latifah answered.

"Exactly all religious books say usury is wrong. So what's the first step to recovery?"

"Get rid of the credit cards."

"No, get rid of the TV."

The kids got excited once again.

"No!!!"

"It's addictive and a waste of time. Read a book, play musical instruments, or simply play sports. You will never see a footballer wearing glasses unless they are sunglasses. Probably don't even read books."

"Any questions in relation to my artistic explanation of budgeting and a happy life."

Rihanna felt uneasy and asked, "Does the preacher ever practice what he preaches?"

"This one does, without even people knowing that he has practiced."

"Are you some kind of new prophet?"

"All good people are prophets and will go to heaven and they will lead a happy and successful life. Look at Hadeeth on success. With every hardship, there is ease – 94:5-6. That means with every problem there are new opportunities and challenges that should be availed and to think out of the box. It's important to know that most successful people think out of the box, like 'Superman' who used to go above the earth to see where in the world there are problems and then focus on the problem. God has used cartoons and movies to show that the hadeeths worked. Each one has been a box office sensation. Unfortunately, Muslims don't either understand or misinterpret the concept behind each hadeeth. With Ladies, Gentleman and great children I rest my case and refer you to not the hadeeths but words of the prophets written on subway walls and tenement halls as sung by Simon and Garfunkel in 'Sound of Silence'. If some are poor then in the tenement halls in housing council complexes people write to express their beliefs. Have you ever been to one? I lived in one."

"No!" everyone replied.

"God forbid you have to live there, but I suggest you walk around and inside the halls and see for yourself what I mean. It's a life changer."

X – 6

The Nephew

Whilst Austin worked in the Middle East, his nephew started to meddle with drugs and after a few years borrowed money to support his family after he lost his full-time job.

He borrowed £10,000 until he found a new job. It never materialized and he ended up being hounded by the drug lord running and ruining Berkshire and Hampshire.

Goodrick, of Waylen Street, Reading, was seen interacting with known drug users at Jesse Terrace, Reading at 5 pm on September 21. The drugs were seized by Thames Valley Police officers and they also took cash and a mobile phone. Goodrick had over £50,000 stashed in the property, privately educated Goodrich pleaded guilty and got two years in jail. His six children suffered immensely in those two years of imprisonment, not only in Goidrich but also because of drug lords looking for money.

When Austin returned from the Middle East he went to visit his ill father and without further ado, the nephew walked in and went straight in to see his grandfather. The nephew was a web developer, which meant nothing to him.

"That's my nephew," Austin thought as he walked right passed them looking worried.

"Is that why you don't kill spiders?"

Rehana asked, "He's a developer isn't he?"

"Is that supposed to be funny?" Austin threw back. The poor attempt at a joke didn't amuse Austin.

Rehana tried again, "You once told me that the two you used to make a telephone out of old tins and string lines when he was six."

Austin took out his mobile phone and said, "Today kids aged seven are making phones in China. Kids of today in U.K should thank their lucky stars."

Rehana scoffed, "We should thank our lucky stars that we are not as smart as we think we are."

"By the way my ex-wife called this afternoon," Austin told her.

Rehana raised a brow, "Is that why you're angry?"

"You know she's crazy," he replied with a shrug.

"Is she still your baby?"

"Not even maybe?"

"How can you say that?" Rehana sent him a glare.

"Because you ignored your cat."

"I was just thinking to myself."

"Did you see her?" Rehana asked to satiate her curiosity.

Austin nodded, "Yes, I saw her." Then asked, "Are you still angry?"

Rehana sighed, "No, I am not angry."

"So shut the door it's cold and come here."

"Is it the cold weather?"

"No, it's just what she said."

"Have you been talking to her?"

"How I am supposed to feel about the things you reveal to her and not me," Rehana asked, an upset look plastered on her face.

"Luckily you're not as smart as you like to think you are."

"Why do you want to talk about it?"

"About why I'm not smart or why she's still crazy?"

"Why is she still crazy it's been over twenty years."

"Lisa was discouraged in love well before she met me."

"In what way?"

Austin sighed, "Her life was in disarray at the age of 18. Well before I met her. She was stumbling around thinking she was falling off the edge of a cliff."

"Do you still want her?" Rehana asked, an eyebrow raised as he waited for him to answer in anticipation.

Austin frowned before he replied, "I want to help her, she's the mother of my children."

"Really, can you ever forget her?"

"Baby, now stop it. I came to see my father and you should know better."

"I know it's hard for me to do, but there is no one for me other than you."

"Baby, I am sorry, I was wrong, I have no alibis. I was acting like a fool and I apologize."

"Look darling just don't look so glum, because you're not dumb, but she thinks you are."

"I can thank my lucky stars that you are here."

"I will always be here for you and if need you pull you out of your grave."

"What if I decide to get cremated?"

"I won't let them. So come here and hold me tight because it's cold in here."

Once the care workers had attended to Austin's father, he entered the room to see his nephew crying.

"What's the matter?" he asked thinking there was something wrong with his father.

"Give him £2000," his father replied.

"Give who £2000?"

"Billy Boy, that's who."

"Why?" Austin asked.

"Just do it, you have plenty it's loose change to you."

His father was bedridden as he had recently fallen over and broke his pelvis.

Austin asked Rihanna to tend to his father and asked Billy Boy to see him outside in the lounge.

"What do you need the money for?"

Billy Boy started to cry.

"You don't know my life."

"I know it's not the same as when you were young."

"I did things wrong and ended up in jail."

"Hang on, this is all news to me for the first time. I always told you not to be a hero. Was it the wrong company?"

"It was a difficult time for me and needed to make money."

"Everyone goes through difficult times but not everyone resolves to sell drugs."

"I needed £10,000 so I borrowed it."

"You know anyone in this country can earn £10000 by merely sweeping floors. Let me talk to your father first about giving you the money."

Austin phoned his elder brother.

He picked up without any preamble and when Austin asked about his nephew, his brother replied, "This evening I have blocked my son on my phone. I can't believe I would do that to him but I can't cope with the relentless texting and calling. He says he owes money to a loan shark but I'm not sure I believe him. He says he borrowed money to buy drugs now he has lost his job and can't pay them. He says he is frightened for his life. After many years of giving him money over and over, I decided some time ago not to give him another penny. I have told him this and explained why but it does not stop him. He threatens to take his own life and self-harm if I don't give him the money and this week this has moved to nasty comments about me."

"Okay, so where did the money go?" asked Austin.

"No idea. He says he is a dead man because he can't pay them and it's my fault!" his brother shouted through the phone. "Not sure how he has concluded that, but it should've been managed better. That lifestyle is so alien and unknown to us and that in itself is frightening."

Austin looked tired and confused, but he had enough strength to reply, "I think you have to trust your instincts and also your resolve. You don't have the money, it may not be true, and it's his responsibility. Blaming you is manipulative and cruel, but you know that. Well done for blocking his calls. There's a limit to what any of us can take and it sounds really positive that you have recognised your limit. However, have you checked whether this is true or just a way of getting money from what he says is a 'stingy father'"

"It was all in the newspaper that Billy Boy went to jail for a couple of years."

"Okay, so why wasn't I informed."

"We had no number and tried your UK number, but it was going on to the answering machine."

"Yes, you're right I had to get a new sim card for Saudi Anyway what's happened has happened and there is little we can do apart from Billy Boy to rebuild his life," Austin concluded, he immediately turned to Rihanna.

"Do you remember I told you I did a stint in prison when I was nineteen?"

"Briefly but I can't remember."

"I was out in jail on a complaint by my ex-wife for rape. They gave me a whole life sentence and I struggled inside as the other prisoners took revenge. I was cornered almost every day after breakfast, lunch, and tea."

"You poor thing."

"However, I never did it, but the ex-wife was clearly cleverer than me."

"How?"

"She simply scratched her private area and made it like I did it."

"How?"

"No idea, I was working in Ipswich at the time and I was staying in a rented room. I was returning after work and about 100 yards away coming from the opposite direction there was a blue light flashing. I quickly took a right turn into the road I was staying."

"That was silly."

"I know but when I looked behind there was another blue light and I went to the side of the road to let the police car take over but instead of going straight on, the car driver waved for me to follow the car." Austin paused for a second, then continued, "The car stopped in the car park of some warehouse. I got out of the car and started apologizing for taking the turn in front of an emergency ambulance."

He sighed before continuing again, "Are you Austin Brady? The arresting police officer said. I said yes."

"I am arresting you in connection with an alleged rape of a female adult." the police officer had said.

"Which female adult?" Austin had asked confused.

"Don't worry you'll find out," the officer replied.

"What now? What about my car?" Austin asked worriedly.

The police officer shrugged, "Don't worry they won't send you a parking ticket in prison."

"You do not have to say anything. But it may harm your defence if you do not mention when questioned something which you later rely on in court. Anything you do say may be given in evidence."

"Ok, what now?"

"Just wait in the police car whilst we search your car."

The policeman handcuffed Austin and he waited in the car.

After a few minutes, a large police transit came and parked next to the police car with blue light flashing.

"You need to go into the van."

"What about my phone?" Austin asked, worried for himself.

"We have it and will remain with us," the police stated simply.

In cases where offences such as rape or sexual assault are alleged, disclosure of the content of messaging on the complainant's mobile telephone often becomes a highly relevant issue. Allegations of this nature are often made by those in a relationship with the suspect or there may be significant dispute about consent.

Those suspected of such offences will often wish to rely upon messaging between the parties but also seek to establish whether there is other evidence on the phone which goes to the credibility of the complainant. Such cases often involve the consumption of alcohol and first-hand evidence of the witnesses.

Once Austin was read out the charges by the Station Sergeant Austin was immediately taken to the cell and then reality hit him and he vomited. Austin was a hard-working family man, with grandchildren and questions remaining in his head to the extent he sat on the edge of the hard fibreglass bed and held his head in head. He knew he had three basic rights, firstly to access free legal advise. Secondly, the right to let someone he has been arrested. Thirdly, the right to look at police codes of practice. So, he asked the arresting officer if he could ring his wife.

The officer responded, "Sorry, but she is the one who made the allegations."

Austin kept quiet and thought the only person in that case who could help him was God and the hadeeth. Also, he knew that he couldn't be kept in a police cell for more than 24 hours without being charged.

After being arrested there were a few options available, no further action, being charged, receiving a caution, or going to the hospital under the Mental Health Act. He decided that going to the hospital was the best option. Austin decided that he would go on a hunger strike and tell the station medical doctor that he wanted to kill himself.

He also asked the doctor who was a muslim to look at the hadeeth for false allegations from his wife. As far as Austin was concerned that was the unwritten law.

"The husband has the right to discipline his wife if she disobeys him in something good, not if she disobeys him in something sinful, because Allah has enjoined disciplining women by forsaking them in bed and by hitting them lightly and if there is any benefit in that when they do not obey."

"So, lightly smacking the bottom is allowed?"

"I presume so, but I wouldn't advise."

"But my wife always smacks her bottom."

"Then we will have a problem."

"Why?"

"It is considered against the law to follow the rights of a husband if any other law other than UK law is applied."

"I can admit to that because when I was at school I used to get into trouble with the teachers as the girls wouldn't let me play with them and so I used to wait until break time and then the one who was rude I used to lift their skirts and smack on their bottom."

"Oh dear, so do you think that was the trigger."

"Not sure, but it was lightly, not a forceful smack. As I was led to believe by the mosque I was allowed to do that. And the teacher used to smack us when we hit things wrong. So, I took it as if a girl was being disrespectful then it was okay to smack them on the bottom."

"I wouldn't actually say that to the police, they'll lick you up and throw the key away."

"Why?"

"Let's just keep to your state of mind at present."

"My state of mind is fine, but I shouldn't be here, possibly I should be in the mental health unit, getting traumatised at the mosque has caused these issues."

"You can't keep blaming the mosque in your mid-fifties."

"I'm actually in my mid-sixties."

"So have harboured these issues for nearly six decades."

"Not sure if they are issues, more application of the hadeeth."

"And do you agree with these?"

"I have to follow the intention and way to fulfill that intention."

"Again, I wouldn't recommend you tell that to the police."

"Are you telling me that I shouldn't claim to be affected by what happened in my childhood?"

"I'm just a doctor, so will recommend a therapy under the Mental Health Act to the Sergeant and let him decide."

When Austin returned to the cell and thought about his nephew and concluded that it was better to claim that he was affected by certain events in his life that determined his upcoming retirement. Leaving the country was a difficult decision, but it would mean he would find peace away from his childhood and the familiarity of England, lie on on beach somewhere, and think of England.

He decided to buy a boat, do it up, and sail to Calais first and see if he could handle the sea, if asked by the coast guards why he was going the other way, he would just say, "Let the immigrants have the UK, the politicians have ruined it."

X – 7

The Sacrificial Lamb

Mount Gerizim, situated near the Palestinian city of Nablus and the biblical city of Shechem, stands as one of two prominent peaks in the vicinity. It delineates the southern edge of the valley where Nablus resides, with Mount Ebal forming the northern boundary.

As one of the loftiest summits in the West Bank, it reaches a height of 881 meters (2,890 feet) above sea level, slightly lower than its counterpart, Mount Ebal.

Notably steep on its northern face and adorned sparsely with shrubbery at its peak, Mount Gerizim hosts a spring that generously yields fresh water further down its slopes. Revered by the Samaritan community, who predominantly inhabit its surroundings, Mount Gerizim holds unparalleled significance as the holiest site on Earth for them.

In biblical accounts, the mountain is referenced as the site where, upon their initial entry into the Promised Land following the Exodus, the Israelites conducted ceremonies of blessings in accordance with the instructions given by Moses.

To the Samaritans, Mount Gerizim holds sacred significance, being esteemed as the chosen site for a holy temple by God, surpassing even Jerusalem's Temple Mount in importance. According to Samaritan tradition, it stands as the most ancient and pivotal mountain globally, rising above the waters of the Great Flood and serving as the initial land upon which Noah's ark came to rest.

Additionally, it is revered as the place where Abraham came close to sacrificing his son Isaac. In contrast, Jewish tradition identifies Mount Moriah, traditionally linked with the Temple Mount, as the site of the near-sacrifice.

Even today, Mount Gerizim remains the focal point of Samaritan religious practice, with Samaritans making pilgrimages to its summit three times annually: at Passover, Shavuot, and Sukkot. Passover is observed by the Samaritans with a traditional lamb sacrifice atop Mount Gerizim. Presently, approximately half of the surviving Samaritan population resides near Gerizim, primarily in the quaint village of Kiryat Luza.

Kiryat Luza, a Samaritan village, and the Israeli settlement of Har Brakha are both located atop the ridge of Mount Gerizim.

Furthermore, besides being examined by contemporary scholarship, this biblical event has attracted significant commentary in the traditional texts of Judaism, Christianity, and Islam.

In the Hebrew Bible, it is recounted that God instructs Abraham to present his son Isaac as an offering. Once Isaac is securely bound to an altar, an emissary from God intervenes, preventing Abraham from carrying out the sacrifice, affirming, "Now I know you fear God." Abraham then notices a ram and offers it as a sacrifice in place of Isaac.

Isaac's demise was never within the realm of possibility – neither in Abraham's understanding nor in God's intentions. God's directive to Abraham was exceptionally clear-cut, and Abraham comprehended it with utmost clarity: Isaac was designated to be "raised up as an offering," with God utilizing the occasion to unequivocally communicate that human and child sacrifice is utterly unacceptable.

This precise interpretation mirrors the understanding of the sages of the Talmud (Taanit 4a) regarding the Akedah. Drawing from the admonition of the Prophet Jeremiah against child sacrifice (chapter 19), they affirm without ambiguity that such abhorrent practices "never crossed God's mind," explicitly referring to the prospect of Isaac being sacrificed.

Despite the disquietude and even horror experienced by readers of this narrative over the ages, there existed no misunderstanding between God and Abraham. The notion of actually carrying out Isaac's death never arose in their contemplations.

Muslims honor and remember Abraham and his son's submission during the days of Eid al-Adha. This festival is marked by those who are able and those undertaking the pilgrimage to sacrifice a ram, cow, sheep, or camel. A portion of the sacrificial meat is consumed by the family, while the rest is shared with neighbors and those in need. Eid al-Adha signifies the culmination of the Hajj pilgrimage to Mecca.

There was a lot that Austin thought about in his retirement whether Rihanna used him as the sacrificial lamb to climb the ladder in the United Nations and she had developed an ego similar to Hitler. He, like her, preferred fruit and vegetables rather than meat, constantly ran his index finger under his nose, drank herbal tea instead of coffee, and hated people smoking in his presence, a short and slim man, like Rihanna. He had a "Messiah Complexity" believing he was chosen to eliminate evil and Jews, but Rihanna had produced a good son trying to take the world over in another way.

On the other side of the Atlantic, Harry had a meeting with an investment company for the vaping industry and he walked into a meeting rather nervous with a hoodie. The board members looked at him but liked what they saw. A young man of twenty had written a business plan and had eighteen freelance workers in his team with no revenue.

He stood in front of a room full of people who would decide what his future would look like and said, "Morning, I'm Harry Brady, I have come here to seek funding for a revolution."

One of the company members asked, "What experience do you have in taking on the government?"

Harry cleared his throat lightly before replying, "My grandfather was a revolutionary cabinet minister and fought against the military rule in a third-world country and my mother's father was Hitler's right-hand man."

"Wow! Is that your motivation?" he asked.

Harry shook his head, "No, it's Mission-Driven Innovation: We're dedicated to fighting underage vaping and fostering sustainability in the industry. Reimagining Recycling: Our goal is a closed-loop system for vaping device disposal to minimize environmental impact. Powered by VusionID: Our cutting-edge technology uses ID verification via our Vusion app to prevent underage use and promote the development of healthier habits. The

Solaris Token Reward: Incentivizing user participation in age-verification and sustainability initiatives."

The company members sitting around the table nodded their heads as they listened. The one at the head of the table said, "That deserves another 'wow'? Doesn't it?"

"I call it 'Annus Horribilis.'" Harry replied.

"Annus Horribilis?"

Harry smiled slightly and said, "In 1992, the British royal family faced a series of scandals, including marital issues involving three of the queen's children, which received significant media attention. Early in the year, Prince Andrew announced his separation from Sarah Ferguson, the Duchess of York. This was followed in April by the divorce of Queen Elizabeth's daughter, Princess Anne, from Captain Mark Phillips. During the summer, the publication of an unauthorized biography of Diana, Princess of Wales, consort to Elizabeth's heir, Prince Charles (later Charles III), exposed details of their troubled marriage, fueling tabloid speculation. Then, in November, a fire caused extensive damage to Windsor Castle. My family suffered in 2018 so that is my year of Annus Mirabilis."

Another member spoke up, "What kind of suffering?"

"My father had a mental breakdown after being scammed for nearly £60k. My mother followed suit in 2019. And I found out I was an atheist in 2020 after the covid pandemic. By watching 'The Theory of Everything.' I watched it four times and every time cried throughout the film," Harry replied.

"Why?"

"The Theory of Everything is the story of the most brilliant and celebrated physicist of our time, Stephen Hawking, and Jane Wilde, the arts student he fell in love with while studying at Cambridge in the 1960s. Little was expected from Hawking, a bright but shiftless student of cosmology after he was given just two years to live following the diagnosis of a fatal illness at 21 years of age."

"How does it affect you?"

"I am also a Physicist at Kings College, London. In the 1960s, Cambridge University student and future physicist Stephen Hawking falls in love with fellow collegian Jane Hawking. At 21, Hawking learns that he has motor neuron disease. Despite this -- and with Jane at his side -- he begins an ambitious study of time, of which he has very little left, according to his doctor. He and Jane defy terrible odds and break new ground in the fields of medicine and science, achieving more than either could hope to imagine."

"I can't see any similarities. You're a good-looking young man."

He had seen the movie enough times to know it like the back of his hand. As he started to speak, the words flew out of his mouth effortlessly.

The movie starts as the Cambridge student Stephen Hawking meets Jane, and although shy at first, eventually they both get close. Stephen soon learns about his illness and decides to shut Jane off from his life. But Jane insists they stay together, knowing the illness will progress and slowly take Stephen away from her. They get married soon after, and Stephen soon graduates from his doctoral study, having more interest in cosmological physics. Jane stands by Stephen as the illness progresses, impairing his locomotion, balance, speech, and even swallowing. They have two children and Stephen's work starts to gain the spotlight. But little by little, Jane starts to lose her spirit, though she doesn't reveal it.

Jane's mother advises her to join the church choir to help fill her spare time so she goes. There she meets the choir's tutor Jonathan. Jonathan gets close to Jane and her family, even with Stephen. He goes as far as being a helping hand for Stephen when the family goes on an outdoor trip. Jane ultimately starts to feel attracted to Jonathan. But Jonathan backs away when friends and families start to whisper. As Jane goes with Jonathan, Stephen goes to watch an opera. But Stephen has an episode and goes into a coma, and the doctors hesitate in doing a tracheotomy on him due to his muscles already having atrophied which means Stephen's ability to speak will be impaired. Jane insists on a tracheotomy, but the family then struggles to communicate with Stephen.

Jane hires a help, Elaine, who quickly suits Stephen's needs while Jane slowly slips away from him. Stephen then gets the robotic speech aid program which helps him a lot. But then Jane reaches her limit and she and Stephen get a divorce. Jane goes on to marry Jonathan. But Stephen calls for Jane, as the first spouse, to accompany him in receiving a title from the Queen.

All of the people sitting at the table listened quietly. When he had finally finished speaking, the head asked curiously, "Why do you think it's like your life?"

Harry shrugged before replying, "I am shy and had a girlfriend at sixteen, who my mother didn't approve of."

"That would be Rihanna Brady?"

Harry nodded, "Yes, the upcoming MP for South Leicester."

"And your father?"

"A civil engineer."

"Good, at least we got that out of the way."

"Above are only sky. Imagine there's no heaven."

"It's easy if you try," Jess interrupted.

Jess was a beautiful brunette who had been observing Harry and writing down in her notebook quietly.

"No he is below us," Harry replied.

"Above us only sky."

"Imagine all the people, living as one. Just living for today."

"Exactly, Like Stephen Hawkings did," Jess commented.

The meeting had transgressed a bit and instead of the usual thirty minutes it had been running for over forty minutes. Since it had taken more time, the meeting was adjourned for a short break. Everyone left except for Jess who looked at Harry curiously.

In the silence, Harry added, continuing the conversation from before, "My father has hemorrhoids and struggles with stopping smoking and has been to herbalists in Birmingham."

"Birmingham, Alabama?" Jess asked.

"Birmingham UK. They are called Annus Herbalists. They make drinks containing a formula by Edwin Smith

Papyrus (1700 BC) and the Ebers Papyrus (1500 BC) recommend astringent lotions containing honey, myrrh, flour, ibex fat, and sweet beer for anal symptoms that are strongly suggestive of symptomatic hemorrhoids. There is no surgical treatment and the Annus Herbalist took advantage and it cost him a fortune. She even took him to a priest who said only faith could heal him."

Jess arched a brow, "Isn't that Austin Brady?"

"Yes, that's my father and he's now trying to sue both the herbalist and the priest."

"I understand, I had a similar experience."

"What hemorrhoids?"

"No, I couldn't conceive," Jess admitted.

"And?"

"The herbalist tried but I couldn't conceive and then she referred me to a Hindu priest."

"Any luck?"

"I conceived, but the priest raped me and I stabbed him in the neck."

Harry's eyes widened, "In Leicester?"

"Yes, how do you know?"

"I live in Leicester and read it in a newspaper, the priest was bi-sexual and was a prominent clubber in the city and was married without children."

"I'm glad you support me."

"He targeted young men and women by offering services on the internet."

"Unfortunately, I was the victim, not the aggressor."

She added, "Mr Shah was in the habit of carrying lots of cash on his person and in his car. After stabbing him, I took his money. His wife came to see me and said he was a "godly figure."

"Depends how one describes 'Godly'," Harry said with a shrug.

"I presume he was pleasing both men and women. However, his wife was undergoing fertility treatment as she couldn't conceive."

"Exactly so he was trying to prove that it wasn't his fault that his wife couldn't conceive," Harry confirmed to Jess.

In India and most Asian countries, it was considered that either the wife or husband was evil when a couple couldn't conceive a child.

"Infertility is a disease or condition of the reproductive system. It is a physical problem, not a psychological one. While relaxing may help you with your overall quality of life, the stress and deep emotions you feel are the result of infertility, not the cause of it. In fact, one or more physical causes are identified in the vast number of infertile couples. So while relaxing, going on vacation, or finding positive ways to de-stress can improve your overall well-being, these lifestyle changes won't solve your infertility problems," said Harry.

"Strictly speaking, infertility is defined as one year of unprotected intercourse without conception. *However*, this does not mean that women over age 35 and those with a history of irregular periods, fibroids, endometriosis, pelvic adhesive disease, ectopic pregnancy, or recurrent miscarriage should wait it out for a whole year. On the contrary, anyone who falls into any of these categories should seek help as soon as they decide the timing is right to start a family. This is also true for men with a history of surgery, infection, or trauma to the genital organs. If either partner has known physical problems that may affect your fertility, don't wait to get an evaluation," clarified Jess.

"So did you conceive with the priest?"

"Yes, and he is now four."

"Why did you keep the baby?"

Jess sighed before replying, "So, I could give his wife some joy in life."

"You mean like a surrogate mother?"

"Exactly, and I see him every three months."

When the assessment officer walked back into the office.

Jess started to read her report back to both Harry and the assessment officer.

"We have discussed with Harry Brady that his vision, research, and development have been great timing and have covered the following: Haris has developed the company based on his dedication and to leverage the beauty of physics and mathematics to tackle and intrinsically use the first principles to solve global and universal problems by unraveling the mysteries of the universe. I recommend an investment of £200k into his company and see the development, production, and implementation of the vaping microchip called 'Idris' and the app called 'Abida' after his grandfather and grandmother's names were met in childhood and recently passed away and he saw them holding hands at an early age. Haris's motivation is driven by personal and professional motivation which as an investment fund is critical and motivates interest in young talent. On a personal note, his father was heavily involved and invested nearly £400k in the family business and when the post office scandal happened some forty years ago, his father was the sacrificial lamb."

Harry was happy with the outcome. Now, it was time for his dreams to come true.

X – 8

Headmistress

The headmistress suffered from angina and was bipolar. She sat there both heads bowed grimly as she grumbled.

"What you grumbling about now?" Ronaldy asked.

"Palestine, they shouldn't have attacked women and children. It's like they are alienating the Muslim population," she replied with a huff.

Ronaldy rolled his eyes, "Don't talk about war and religion, it depresses me."

"If we don't talk about it, then how do we work out how to fix it?"

"So? As one war finishes another one starts. It's never-ending," he shrugged carelessly.

"Austin did say it was the start of the end of the world," she mused.

Ronaldy sat up straighter and turned to look at the headmistress, "Him? What did he know?"

"He knew a lot, but you wouldn't listen."

Ronaldy sighed, "You can because you have two heads four ears, and two brains."

The headmistress scoffed, "He also said he had chicks everywhere."

"Not those types but horrible girls who wrecked my marriage."

"I don't think Austin was inclined that way as I never saw him with anyone. He explained to me that he trains young girls so they are independent from their partners."

"He was always touching them."

"I think it was the other way round."

By offering paid training, Austin used to hire the girls out to construction companies at a lower rate than normally qualified designers using AutoCAD at a third of the cost and winning contracts for design and build. The girls were grateful and he made a handsome profit.

"He lost all his money employing these women as they used to go the pub every day."

"I think you're overthinking, he made money and used to claim against tax the visits."

"So where did the money go?"

"He put the money into research and development but the solution cost three times more than he expected because you were in charge. Any girls applying you used to scare them. He always said that Islam promoted the teaching and training of women so they become self-sufficient."

"More like training and trading women."

"Why do you always think badly of him?"

"Because he is bad. There's no doubt about it."

"You say the same thing about me."

"Austin created you didn't he?"

"He didn't create me, he modified me for a purpose to put children playing PS Games."

"And did your modifier succeed?"

"Okay, he didn't succeed, but it's better than not trying."

"He was going on about Moulana Superprayer somewhere in Canada and said in his death bed to go and see him."

"I can't stay like this and we need to go."

"Oh it's easy for you to say but it's far far away."

"It's only a bit far."

"Bit far, did you say bit far?"

"Across the Atlantic, that's all."

"Let's see what my son has to say."

Ronaldy rubbed a sphere and a hologram appeared.

"Mum, can you leave me alone, please? I am in the middle of sending rockets into space."

"Just like your father, wasting good money after bad."

"It's not wasting money, just imagine if I germinate a plant on a planet or meteor then we can send people there."

"What about the Headmistress?"

"Whose Headmistress?"

"Your Dad's creation. Look over there in the corner."

"My Gods of Zigog. What has he done?"

"You know how he used to tell stories well Headmistress is the result of that."

"I know he used to make up great stories and characters but I think he went a bit far on this one."

"Not only Headmistress have two heads, but she is also bipolar with a fat bottom."

"Maybe something to do with the ex-wife."

"When everything fell apart he replicated the mother hen as how he saw her and always had a hand up her bottom to check the egg formation."

"Well, he was a failed doctor," said Harry.

"More like a failed dictator."

"Anyway, what are you up to and upset about? I know that look."

"The rockets keep blowing up. I have spent a hundred million and only went up to a mile at the most."

"Ironic as it sounds. Have you tried chicken poop with methane?"

"Mum!"

"It is quite explosive but cheap."

"Mum, stop it, I have too much on my mind to argue with you. No wonder Dad called you Tangent Point."

"I always wondered why he called me TP."

"Because you focus on the issue for a split second and then go off on a tangent."

"You're are exactly like your Dad."

"What focused and dignified?"

"No, a prat."

"You also called him a funny guy. That I agree with him was fun to be with."

"No, I meant his way with me."

"You mean men?"

"Yes, men."

"Your command of English isn't still perfect."

"His command of French wasn't good either."

"Are we going to start talking about your grandfather being the illegitimate child of Napoleon again? We've been through that many times. It was just Dad's way of getting attention."

"I know I have the skin colour of mocha and wear dark lipstick but I was never French."

"Then I remember he once said your father was Hitler's right-hand man and people started running around the shop serving you like crazy. He was funny. I wish he was alive."

"He can be," Headmistress said looking deeper and suicidal.

"See what you do to people!"

"And hens and men, all peoples."

"I think you need to take some English lessons."

"There read this, I couldn't understand what he wrote."

Harry looked at the blood-stained piece of paper.

"Who is Moulana Superprayer?"

"I think that's one of his sons from a previous marriage. He wears the Liverpool kit under an Islamic dress. That's the only way to recognize him."

"And where does this Moulana live."

"Canada. He teaches young kids to support Liverpool and when he has time he flies around the world telling kids to support Liverpool and raise money to install water wells in poor countries."

"What's wrong with that?"

"And he's always laughed at his Dad's jokes."

"Most people did."

Across the Atlantic, in the Northern Hemisphere, a little town called "Yukon".

A giggling man was practicing with a witch's broom. In front of him was a full-sized doll that wore red lipstick and dark glasses. He poked it twice in the stomach and then swung the broomstick around the head and it went flying across the lounge, where three children sitting in Liverpool kit looked in amazement, mouths wide open.

"There that's what I do to people who don't support Liverpool."

"Dad? Is there something you need to talk about? It's quite serious what you did."

"No, anyone supporting Liverpool is a trigger for me. Like my Dad he supported Everton and it caused endless arguments between my mum and him, eventually leading to divorce. He wouldn't compromise, it was either Everton or no one because at birth I was a blue baby, ironically and Dad said I was the chosen one, the special one."

"What's a blue baby?"

"It's called 'Cyanosis' which is due to low oxygen levels in the blood. Dad always said that because my mom was overweight and her stomach was suffocating me during pregnancy I should support Liverpool."

"So, how did you get superpowers?" Yousef asked as he played with the Power Rangers.

"I worked hard, exercised with a broomstick and played football every day, got into a local cricket club and took five wickets in a cup match, and then got dropped in the final. I was a victim of racism and I stopped playing after that."

"So what did you do after that?" asked Aliyah.

"I decided to study law at Queen's Mary College, London, and finally after fours got a Master in International Law."

"And after that?"

"Worked on my football franchises until I met your mum."

"Had to get away from the UK because your granddad met a younger woman and had kids. So I decided to specialize in superpowers and superpowers. As soon as I put on my Islamic dress I get to do super prayers that give me strength and teach me discipline. Once the prayers are over I take the dress off and get super powerful. I tie the dress around my waist and I can fly anywhere in the world."

"Can you show us please, please Papa?"

"Of course, but there is a favor you must do for me."

"We'll do anything."

"Anything?"

"Never tell anyone about me or my superpowers and it's a secret between me and you kids. A family secret."

"So, when can we see you fly?"

"Soon, very soon after Ramadhan."

During Ramadhan, the Moulana Superprayer used to switch off and concentrate on his prayers and charity. Out of the vast wealth of dealing on stocks and shares and advising International Companies agree to terms and conditions of the contract. Moulana Super Payer did very well until suddenly his wife passed away, leaving three children under six without a father. He had decided to use his wealth to look after his children.

As a widower, he was married to his beliefs and all the religions in the world. He didn't discriminate against anyone as he suffered racism at an early age in cricket, football, and various clubs he visited in West London. Ramadan was a very special month between the full moon and the new moon. He prayed for the whole world as he knew the Almighty never discriminated against others and the difference between good and evil. There were two simple requirements for improving anyone's life, firstly the intention and secondly perfecting the way of fulfilling that intention.

When a Muslim decided to pray, he thought, he would recite the intention and then he would perform the prayer based on a set of instructions. This he applied vigorously and studiously with the aim that the Almighty set out those two basic instructions. Having a passion for boats he named his daughter "Dignity."

Dignity looked closely at her father, including the Islamic dress and the Liverpool FC kit.

"It can't be all bad a Liverpudlian Moulana Superhero."

The Moulana smiled.

"I'm not a superhero, I have committed a major sin."

"Like what?"

"A few years ago, I was a bad man and ran into a bit of money trouble. I took your mum on a romantic date, but things got out of hand due to my financial situation."

The father took his eldest daughter to a glass-fronted cabinet. Dignity looked closely at a collection of weapons used by eighteenth-century freedom fighters including a thick bamboo stick, with a twist of the stick, which became a knife, along with various knives and knuckle dusters.

"These all belong to your mum as she was interested in weaponry used by Freedom Fighters. She got involved with Freedom Fighter but she wanted a strong man, rather an educated type."

The father then guided his daughter to another room, where there were colored bottles with liquid in them.

"These are from bad old days when I drank heavily and then took your mother's life."

"Is that it?"

"Yes, and every day I regret killing her and dissolving her body in sulphuric acid. I couldn't see my children in Somalia with a freedom fighter."

"So no cops and robbers?"

"Not as a villain, but as a hero I should help the victims."

"I bet you can save the world."

"I couldn't save my marriage, let alone the world."

"Will you be having tea with the Queen of England?"

"It's the king now."

Dignity didn't believe him, as he'd never known her father to be apart from his children. He never ventured out much anymore but to his boat moored in Stewart River. There he would hide his art collection, just in case the police finally caught up with him. It was actually his wife's art collection that he hid from any investigation.

"Papa, what happened to Mana's cartoons?"

"What cartoons?"

"The ones she used to love."

"Those were painted by Lowry."

"Lowry?"

"He developed a distinctive style of painting and is best known for his urban landscapes peopled with human figures, often referred to as "matchstick men. He painted mysterious unpopulated landscapes, brooding portraits, and unpublished "marionette" works, which were only found after his death. He was fascinated by the sea, and painted pure seascapes, depicting only sea and sky, from the early forties. There was a song made after him. They all said his paintings were dull. His paintings hang up on the walls next to the great artists of them all, even Mona Lisa takes a bow. And Lowry left us matchstick men and matchstick cats and dogs. Destiny looked at a tie that was set in a glass box that had an industrial area printed on it which her father used to wear to meetings." He took a deep breath before continuing Destiny, I need you to understand that you mustn't talk about this again, and as you are the eldest you must explain to the other children so they understand."

"I will papa, if my mum was bad enough to leave a kind gentleman like you then I will support you. I am sure you did your best."

"That's why after seven days of her death, God gave me certain powers which frightened me, similar to Prophet Mohammed got frightened when God told him to read and write for the first time."

"Most people say it was hallucinations due to extreme heat in the cave, but you do not believe them and understand God's miracles. God likes simple and uncomplicated people and there is only one race – the human race."

"What my mother did was unforgiving and craft like 'The Road Runner' and tried to kill you and afterward he could not stop the Road Runner because his creator always helped him. That's how I look at God. As my savior against evilness. The coyote will never win."

"That's the best explanation I have ever heard and maybe one day you may get superpowers by offering super prayers. "

"I will Papa, I want to be like you. A gentle person at home and hurt evil. That's what God wanted us to do and it was his test against the human race to differentiate between good and bad. Eventgoid overcomes bad by giving an individual superpowers. Unfortunately, one superhero isn't enough to over the evil, there should be an army of superheroes or heroines ready to be called up against an evil world. When God said after creating Earth, 'It's good enough and the word enough was the clue to evil sections of humanity and it's up to us the believers and good people to overcome the bad." Destiny stared into her father's eyes.

"Let's find those superheroes that are struggling every day in their own trying to stop evil and build an army."

Destiny smiled back with a red beam coming from her fake bindi on her forehead.

X – 9

Mentali

In a weird way, Moulana Superprayer didn't like Ronaldy. As his stepmother, there were times when she complicated issues between him and his father. His real mother never re-married and she was assigned to loneliness after the kids left the nest.

During the Gaza war, his mother became too involved and fought in the street with non-muslims. She would shout at them and throw stones pretending them to be hand grenades and she would shout,

"How do like it when someone is hit by rubble from an Israeli attack?"

They ignored her since most people couldn't careless. However Austin suggested that the children should buy their mother a toy AK47 with plastic bullets, and they did, but it led to the neighbors complaining she was shooting their cat and scaring their aged mother.

When the doctor suggested that she be put in a care home, they agreed. On her first day there, she saw a man pretending to be Thomas The Tank Engine. There was another who thought he was Iron Man and covered himself with spoons and forks. Austin used to call her 'Mentali' and when she was sanctioned under the Mental Health Act, Mentali used to fight with both men and she won every time.

Once when Mentali was spending time in the common are, she heard Iron Man say to Thomas, "It's not how much we've lost, it's how much we have left. We have to beat her one day. She's one hell of a control freak."

Thomas replied, "I think it's best to regroup and refurbish ourselves with better armour."

Mentali used to watch them with barely disguised annoyance and returned to her room as she was writing a book about her ex-husband and how he stopped being a BBC correspondent on international events. She was a woman denied freedom because of culture values. She spent the next two chapters on how they met their wedding night and the honeymoon.

They met through a family friend, but they never hit it off from the start. At the wedding, she sat on the bed with her feet on the bed. Her husband, Mangal was an engineer. He was an atheist and very open-minded.

On the other hand, Mentali had a closed mind. Mangal always waited for the facts to be revealed and then used to make a decision. He would take different cultures, ideas, and perceptions to evaluate a response. That's why their relationship struggled right from the start. Open-minded, he would question everything and everyone, and if there was a disagreement he would search for the root cause of the problem.

The wedding night didn't go as planned and Mangal questioned whether he had made the right decision in choosing the new bride. He thought about all the events leading up to the wedding night.

That's what Mentali wrote in the book. She was aware of the facts but had trouble putting them in writing. It was her life as a teenager and when she looked back to those times it was with a sense of shame. She thought about something she could've done, something she could've said, but eventually, the parents just blamed that 'she was misunderstood' and that was why failed her A'Levels.

Eventually gaining access to a college, she enrolled in a degree program for mentally impaired teenagers.

During this time, Iron man was doing his own thinking and decided to order carbon fibre sheeting. It would prepare him for the next predicted assault and Ronaldy knew that she had just enough time to get Moulana Superprayer to bring back Austin from death. After the seventh day of the 7th month, the prayer had to be performed. The potion was to be used by the 7th hour.

"What time is it now?" Mistress asked, feeling a bit grey.

"Why do you need the time for?" the grey wolf asked.

Mistress paced around restlessly, "It's time that was important to my creator."

"Who? God?" the grey wolf asked with a huff.

"No," the Mistress shook her head, "Austin Brady."

Two eyes stared, cold and silent looking at both the wolf and Headmistress.

"We all fade to grey, whoever created us," said Rundy the wolf.

"We all hear noises from our distant memories. I just remember my creator's voice."

"What's that voice?"

"My creator, saying that he is sorry."

"He must be grey and old now."

"He is a very shade of grey, like clouds on a drizzly morning. Wishing his life was that long so he didn't mess with my mum. Sometimes I wished I had run away when he argued with my mum."

"Did he argue after you were born?"

"Yes, I was born on the 7th hour of the 7th day of the 7th month after 7 other chicks."

"I'd never believed he could do the same to your mum as he did to mine."

"The arguments drove into my heart and caused a lot of pain. I lost the will to fight and couldn't see the light."

"How did your mum cope?"

"She would hold me tight so I could sleep at night."

"I bet it ended in tears," commented Rundy the wolf.

"He abused her tears for years. How come you know so much?"

"He did it, my mum."

"Where you DNA modified too?"

"Yes."

"But you look fine."

"Haven't you noticed my two tails?"

"Oh."

"And I can't howl. Instead, I like to laugh like a hyena."

"That's not bad. I presume he wanted to experiment on mammals first and then birds."

Both Rundy and Headmistress walked through the wood aware that they only had 2 hours to find Moulana Superprayer. The Moulana had no telephone contact as he wanted to live off the grid.

"'Off-the-grid' describes both buildings and lifestyles crafted to function independently, without relying on public utilities. While traditionally associated with disconnecting from the electrical grid, the concept extends to other services such as water, gas, and sewer systems. This approach can range from individual residences to small communities. Embracing off-the-grid living fosters self-sufficiency, particularly beneficial in remote areas beyond the reach of conventional utilities. It also appeals to those seeking to minimize their environmental footprint and reduce living expenses. Generally, an off-grid structure must generate its own energy and provide potable water, while also managing food, waste, and wastewater," said Rundy.

"I presume he had to after his children didn't want to go to school. He agreed it was easier to teach them at home, they didn't have to venture out in the cold freezing temperatures. He wanted them to have access to fresh air and open play areas in the summer," the headmistress replied.

"You know a lot about the family. I was asked by Austin to keep an eye on them as because of Austin, Moulana SuperPrayer became a religious follower of all religions. He was brought up by him."

"And will he fix me?" asked the Headmistress.

"If that's what Austin said. Do you have the letter?"

"Yes."

"How much time have we got left?"

"77 minutes."

"Better speed up them."

"How far is it now?"

"It's not far at all, but we have to cross the river."

"This not the same as the wolf, goat, and cabbage crossing the river by boat is it?"

"Not at all, but there is the lamb that normally crosses the river as well as the grass is over greener on the other side."

"What about the farmer?"

"That's the Moulana. He normally comes across on his boat," explained Rundy the wolf.

"Any issues in the past?"

"Last time it was chaos. We had myself, two bags of cabbage and potatoes from Costco and the lamb. I kept telling Moulana I wouldn't eat the lamb as I am genetically modified, but he wouldn't listen."

"Godsake Rundy, here I will remain with two heads for ever, and you are talking about riddles."

"Let's just get to the crossing point and try and convince Moulana that we are genetically modified apart from the lamb, show him the letter, and maybe we can all cross to gather to save time. What is the treatment anyway?"

"Potion made by Ronaldy and needs to have that mixed with lamb dropping, my droppings, and your droppings, and then two powdered paracetamols."

"But, I've already been today. So that might be difficult."

"It's okay, I bought some laxatives. My life is at stake and Austin's return to life to sort out the world's problems of catastrophic failure to live in peace."

"Why do believe Austin will solve the problems?"

"We were very close to each other and used to sit on the doorsteps singing Ebony and Ivory' which I used to look forward to after supper, have a fag and that bought pleasure to his simple life."

"So why did he fail?"

"He caught chicken pox because his hand was always up my mum's bum messing about with other chicks. Others were fine, I presume I was the black sheep of the family."

"Same here, he was always messing about with my mum and the other unborn pups were fine, I was the faulty one."

"Maybe not, maybe you're the perfect one."

"That's hard to believe."

"No, you are placid, and gentle just like Austin was. The two tails are to signify the difference. I bet all the pups are still wild?"

"Yes, they tease me terribly."

"Well, there you are then. He wanted you to be different."

"How did he make me 'differently'?"

"No idea, but he has a book which Ronaldy keeps safe in the Castle."

"Have you ever seen it?" Rundy asked as he stopped walking.

"I have seen Ronaldy take it out to test on the frogs in the swamp."

"What happened to frogs?"

"They produced loads of tadpoles in the swamp which was a swimming pool. Once they became frogs they started to come into the castle during the winter. Soon North Wales will be over run by frogs. I think she couldn't tell the difference between a toad and a frog personally."

"What's the difference?" asked Rundy.

"Frogs have smooth, slimy skin and have long legs. Toads have warts and dry skin and short legs and crawl everywhere. We need the legs of both the frogs and toads for the magic potion."

"So did you get them?"

"Yes, they are in my rucksack."

"You look like a bomber with that rucksack."

"It was Ronaldy's old rucksack which I cut down to size."

"Who's CFC?"

"The blues – Chelsea Football Club."

"You mean soccer?"

"Yeah- The best club with Jose Mourhino."

"Is he Italian?"

"No, he's a Portuguese with a lot of passion and common sense."

"Is he the special one?"

"Yeah, incredibly special. The chosen one and he was. He had a great art collection which he treasured at home. In a world of all problems and wars, football provides a distinct distraction. I remember Austin used to go nuts when Everton played Liverpool."

"Did you know that Moulana supports Liverpool?"

"Liverpool isn't the same team without Dalglish or Keegan."

"Or Tommy Smith."

"How old are you then?" Headmistress asked.

"Sixty plus. Thanks to Austin."

"What?"

"I remember a lot of wars and catastrophes. I also remember the first personal computer, called Kenbak -1"

"The world is more hostile these days. Aren't you going to ask how old I am?"

"I never ask a chick her age, Austin said it was rude. If a chick likes you she will tell her age herself."

"54. I am 54."

"Hang on a minute. If I am sixty-four, how old was Austin when he was messing around with DNA?"

"I think he was 14. Apparently, he was a spotty teenager, shy and bored."

"It's better to be messing with DNA rather than drugs and alcohol."

"Very true. At least we get to live longer."

"Do you think that's a good idea?"

"Not really, maybe thousands of thousands of years ago when people were more placid and pleasant."

"True, I blame all the fizzy drinks, the internet and alcohol. People have gone crazy."

"During the years of the early prophets, people lived longer."

"There was no electricity, no internet or mobile phones. When electricity was found life has become fast and people can't cope with it."

"Benjamin Franklin."

"Who?"

"He invented electricity." Replied Headmistress.

"I know electricity has always been there in the clouds and fish. So somehow nature gives the clues but we walk right past it."

"You mean likes eels?"

"Yes, even before electricity was invented, Greeks used to tell patients with headaches and gout to touch an electric fish in order to give them a shock hoping to cure them."

"Franklin sold all his possessions to fund the research into finding electricity. He realised that although electricity is a danger it is the most useful invention in history, but God shows that electricity is dangerous, and that went on to power microprocessors and computers that are now a threat to humans. The Internet can be dangerous and it can be beneficial."

Walking towards the river where Rundy and Headmistress saw the boat across the river, they saw a lamb grazing in the distance. When the lamb saw them the lamb came towards them. The boat started to move towards them and Headmistress looked at her watch.

"Just over twenty minutes and we will be okay."

The Searay express boat made its way across the river. A family-friendly vessel, the Searay Express Cruiser SRV260 8.2 boasts six berths. Powered by 2x Mercruiser 4.2 mpi 220 inboard engines with 440hp, it has logged only 122 hours of operation. While the left engine starts and engages smoothly, the right engine requires a fuel pump replacement. Additionally, its lower shift cable is seized, preventing engagement. The boat performed flawlessly on previous outings, but a lapse in regular maintenance led to this issue—a reminder of the importance of periodic checks on a vessel.

Following a refit, the interior features new trim. Its electrical system operates on a 12/24V configuration, supported by three batteries, though the auxiliary battery struggles to hold charge. However, it functions well when the boat is running or connected to shore power. Equipped with a 600-liter petrol tank and a 40-liter drinking water tank, the boat offers ample resources for extended voyages.

Moulana brought it from an old woman whose husband was diagnosed with cancer and she needed the money for his treatment. Primarily bought it for his three kids and they decided to daily take the lamb across the river to their house and then drop the lamb back to feed itself. They called him "Bakri."

By the time the boat moored on the other side of the river, both Headmistress and Rundy could see the Moulana and the kids on the boat. They both started to walk faster as if he was expecting them.

"There he is our savior," said the Headmistress.

"Am I glad to see him," Rundy followed through.

"Let's not count the chickens before the eggs hatch," the Headmistress said giggling whilst Rundy looked dissipated.

As the boat moored, the lamb started to move towards it.

One by one the kids jumped off it. Hakim was only just over one and Moulana carried him off. He yawned as he saw the wolf, the chicken and the lamb, not realising it was a situation for the riddle to be solved.

Rundy saw Moulana and then turned back to the Headmistress who had a serene smile on her face as she said, "To love is to receive a gift from heaven."

A

Austin had driven over 400 miles from Cumbria to Northampton for the weekend only to find an empty house. He assumed that Rihanna and Harry had gone shopping or better still, they might be a surprise for him.

He did not mind the quit though, so he lounged back on his couch and waited for their return. It was almost an hour later when Harry rang the doorbell. Austin opened up the door for him to see that Harry was carrying a painting with him.

Austin raised a brow and asked, "That looks good. Where did you do this?"

Harry smiled at him sheepishly before saying, "Hospital, it's supposed to be a secret."

Austin raised a brow, "What kind of secret?"

"The operation," Harry replied nonchalantly with a shrug.

Austin squinted at Harry, trying to see whether he was actually telling the truth but nothing could be told by his poker face. With a shake of his head, Austin poked his head out of the front door to look for answers regarding his son's suspicious behaviour. He saw a car driving away fast in the dark and Rihanna walking very slowly towards the house. He recognised the car straight away as belonging to her younger sister living around the corner.

Austin said nothing as he left the threshold of his front door. He didn't go to meet Rihanna but went back into the living room where he started pacing up and down with his hands clasped in front of him. He waited until Rihanna finally made her way back into the house.

She closed the door behind her and folded her arms across her chest as she slowly turned to face Austin. "I thought you weren't coming back this weekend," she said, taking a step closer.

Austin sighed, "I have been coming back every weekend for the last two years, it's you who hasn't been here on many occasions. Have I ever questioned you?" he shook his head then because he knew that showing his frustration to his wife most of the time was futile. "Anyway, where have been and why are you walking slowly?"

Rihanna sighed as she walked slowly into the living room and gingerly sat on the couch. She looked everywhere but at Austin when she replied, "I miscarried the baby, I fell down the stairs. Now I'm tired and the doctor told me to rest."

Austin was surprised by the news, but then why hadn't any of them called him to tell him the news? He should know if his wife was having this kind of an emergency. "Didn't the doctor tell you to tell the truth?" he asked, voice bordering on sounding suspicious.

"What do you mean?" Rihanna asked, confused about his line of questioning.

"I haven't seen any blood on the stairs," Austin said, coming to stand in front of her so that he could tell whether she was telling the truth or not.

"I got my sister to clean it up with Vanish," Rihanna told him nonchalantly.

Austin huffed and shook his head before saying, "Okay, suppose I believe you. Can you show me the discharge form from the hospital?"

Rihanna was quiet for a few moments. The silence between them was tense as Austin kept glaring at her but she refused to look his way as she stared angrily at a single point. But then Rihanna scoffed and turned to look into his eyes angrily before blurting out, "No, you killed the baby!"

Austin reeled away in shock. How could that be possible? He was not even here when it happened so how could she put all the blame on him? Once the shock left his body, he looked at Rihanna accusingly and loudly said, "What? How? I was over 400 miles away!"

Rihanna bit her lips harshly, looking like she would rather be anywhere than here, being questioned by Austin just after she had a miscarriage. However, she also knew that this was a conversation that they needed to have. With newly found determination, she squared her shoulders and firmly replied, "Stress of you womanising, drinking, and smoking."

Austin scoffed loudly, marvelling at the nerve of his wife at having made such a decision without telling or consulting him at all. "That is a lie," he stated loudly because he knew his wife very well, "And even so, it doesn't give you the exclusive right to terminate the baby without consulting me. You're not God."

Rihanna arched a brow at him and asked sarcastically, "Are you?"

"A father and husband is the living God. That's what religion says," Austin replied with conviction.

"Austin," Rihanna sighed, looking like she did not want to talk further on this topic, "What are you going to do now?"

Austin sighed, pinching the bridge of his nose because there was so much that he could say but he did not feel like confronting Rihanna any longer. He took a deep breath in to calm himself down before replying, "I feel like going back up to the bedsit to think about what's happened. Get my boat out and go west."

"Aren't you going to grieve with us?" Rihanna asked.

"With Harry maybe but not you as you and your sister, who decided without an inkling of thought for both of us. These are life-changing decisions that don't just affect you but other people as well. My mum always said if a woman makes a decision behind a husband's back then she's capable of anything. I should've listened to my mum," he replied to her, voice dripping with contempt.

As Austin talked, Rihanna's anger grew until it reached a boiling point. To hurt him even further, she spitefully replied, "I also told the doctor you raped me."

Austin scoffed, "That just confirms my mum's comments. I am going back I don't want another regret-fuelled weekend."

With that said Austin walked away and out of the house. He was thinking of going up to bed but now he did not even want to remain in the same house as her. There were limits to some things and it bothered Austin that she had not thought to tell him about what had happened. He got back into his car and headed west towards Cumbria, driving erratically at times. The entire way, he could not help but think about what had transpired. If he hadn't managed to come back today, what would she have told him?

He doesn't know how they had gotten to this point in their relationship where they didn't trust each other when it had started so sweetly. He didn't know where they had gone wrong.

It wasn't fair to him that such big decisions were being made in his family and he, the head of the family, was not being consulted. What was the point in calling them a family anyway?

Once Austin reached the bedsit, he didn't enter it to sit and think, instead, he went straight to the boat and started sailing in the middle of the night. It wasn't the first time he was sailing alone or at night, but it was the first time he was doing this with so many distracting thoughts.

He wanted to forget about what had happened for a while because it was not doing him any favours except for making him angry. Austin rowed slowly, feeling the slight breeze on his heated skin which made the night seem happier. There were no sounds around him except for the gentle swish of the lake, the odd chirping of a bird or insect, and his own breathing. The moment was peaceful, away from all the worries of the world. It was dark all around him and within that darkness was hidden the world that was full of hunger and deception.

In the world out there, everyone was out to get each other. They only worried about themselves and what they could achieve even if it meant hurting others in the process.

In a small boat, Austin was the captain of his own destiny, dwindling in a far, far away ocean. There was no one around to hurt him or deceive him. He had been there many times in his dreams and in reality, trying to have some semblance of peace in his otherwise chaotic world. The peace gave him a lot to think about and wonder about.

Once the boat was on the open ocean, he could see a bank of black clouds hovering above him and he put the sails up. The weather could change any minute so he was not taking any chances of getting stuck way far ahead.

As he remained in one spot, he could not help but notice the wind picking up suddenly. Little raindrops started to fall where he was. It wasn't raining heavily where he was, but he saw the clouds showering upon the ocean floor up ahead. There was a sudden crackle up in the sky and a bolt of lightning narrowly missed the boat.

Normally, Austin would have flinched if not for his distracted thoughts of the baby being aborted by Rihanna. His mind jolted with bursts of anger as he swigged a bottle of whiskey. He had endured pain and laughter in his life, but the deception could never be explained even by God.

Perhaps his feelings would have been different if he had been present and seen what happened, or if Rihanna had been truthful since everything started, but she had only told him when Austin had caught them coming home.

He scoffed out loud and took another swig of the bottle. Like his sleeping pattern, the boat moved haphazardly away from the true line of travel. Austin watched and did nothing as it went further and further. He believed God would help him endure the pain and the storm. He looked up to see the clouds were breaking with the sun slowly peeking through. It seemed like the weather was clearing the more he moved further. Autin's mouth twitched up from one side, in a sort of half-smile, but then his attention was caught by something else. He saw a crow flying from up ahead and then it started descending with speed towards the boat. He sat there, enraptured by the display of nature and God in front of him.

He knew the significance of the crow in religion. The crow brought messages from the spiritual world and symbolised new beginnings, transformations, prophecies, and freedom.

He wondered what all of it meant and why he was experiencing such things. Was it because he had gotten such painful news that now God was trying to tell him that it was all going to be alright?

He didn't know what to make of the sign. Confused and tired, Austin kept his eyes on the crow, only to realize that it was a single crow which normally meant bad luck or death. However, the crow was gazing at him and then started to follow him as the boat moved, meaning that he had to use his wisdom and experience to overcome the problems he was facing.

Before he knew it, the boat had hit land and Austin struggled overboard to see what was around him. There were a lot of bottles surrounding him. He didn't know where they had come from and why they were here, except that they had come to surround the boat as he reached the shore. He was just another castaway, a man lost at sea, a lonely man, with no one there but him. No one to help him out or try to understand how he was feeling.

Would he be rescued out of his despair? He should've known from the start that Rihanna was made by God to break his heart. The bottles reminded him that they must have come from somewhere, all looking for a new home. Austin looked up and in the distance saw a lighthouse. Slowly, he got up from the boat and stepped out. The water splashed around him as he started to walk towards the lighthouse, but after a few steps, his legs gave way. He kneeled on the ground and rested for a while, realizing that not only did his legs feel weak, but his whole body felt like it had no energy. Suddenly, he had the sudden urge to look up, and he saw the most beautiful eyes. There was a woman standing in front of him and she offered her hand to help him up.

Without thinking much, he gave her his hand, and she helped him up, then started to take him towards the lighthouse. On the way, he wrapped his arm around her waist gently, so he could take her support. But as they walked, Austin could not help but feel pain in his right shin. He stopped to look down and saw that it was bleeding. The woman stopped to look at the wound and then promptly took her skirt and ripped a piece to smother the wound. Her hands softly caressed his leg as she helped in stopping the bleeding.

"I hope you can stop the bleeding in my heart," Austin remarked, voice feeling gravelly.

"Do you see all those bottles? They all had messages on them of loneliness and despair," the woman spoke, her voice sweet as honey.

"And I presume you answered them all?" Austin asked, looking at the woman with keen interest.

"No, I can't read or write. I was hoping you could help me," the woman said with a slight smile on her face.

"I have just come from Cumbria, slack jaw and not much to say," Austin said with a shrug.

"Is that where women claw and men plunder?" the woman asked curiously.

"No, that's Wellingborough," Austin smirked.

The woman asked, "Where's that?"

"Northamptonshire. I am 64 full of muscles. Even I plunder now and then," he chuckled.

"When did you last plunder?" the woman asked with a raise of her brow.

Austin hummed thoughtfully before replying, "Every time I see a beautiful lady, like now."

The woman smiled now, wide and bright, "Wounded and charming, just the way I like them. Let's get you inside, warmed up, showered up, and bedded."

She helped him towards the lighthouse and Austin wondered if she was the sign given to him by God.

Available worldwide from Amazon
and in all good bookstores

Michael Terence Publishing

www.mtp.agency

mtp.agency

@mtp_agency

Printed in Great Britain
by Amazon

43541856R00101